THE HANDGUN IN PERSONAL DEFENSE

THE HANDGUN IN PERSONAL DEFENSE

BY
R. K. CAMPBELL

MERRIL PRESS

BELLEVUE, WASHINGTON

The Handgun in Personal Defense © **2005**

By R.K. Campbell

All Rights Reserved

The Handgun in Personal Defense is published by Merril Press, P.O. Box 1682, Bellevue, WA 98009. Additional copies of this book may be ordered from Merril Press at $15.00 each. Phone: 425-454-7009. Book designed by Tiffany Lindsay.

FIRST EDITION

LIBRARY OF CONGRESS CATALOGING-IN-PUBLICATION DATA

Campbell, R. K. (Robert K.), 1958-
    The handgun in personal defense / by R. K. Campbell.-- 1st ed.
    p. cm.
    ISBN 0-936783-42-7
        1. Pistols. 2. Pistol shooting. 3. Self-defense. I. Title.

TS537.C24 2004
613.6'6'0284--dc22

2004057865

PRINTED IN THE UNITED STATES OF AMERICA

CONTENTS

INTRODUCTION

The handgun is alternately feared, revered, despised and idolized. No other personal defense implement evokes the emotional response the handgun does. Arguably, the pistol is not an implement of war but of civilian defense. Since many world organizations attempt to assume responsibility for their citizens safety, they also limit handgun ownership. The disarming of citizens results in a nation of subjects, not citizens, at best. At worst, they are slaves. I cannot argue that handguns do not figure into crime and mischief, of course they do. I have documented hundreds of criminal attacks. But the use of handguns by citizens in defense of their person or home far outweighs the offensive criminal use. The hero cop shooting it out with armed felons is the exception. Frail females or elderly persons are often those who benefit the most from handgun defense. Our freedom of choice in arming ourselves has been attacked, but seems safe in the foreseeable future. I hope freedom rings in the rest of the world as well. If the right to bear arms and the human right to self defense is curtailed, we face the prospect of a different and difficult future.

RKC

CHAPTER ONE
THE HANDGUN'S PLACE

Long ago I wrote a scathing editorial to my local paper. It was never published. The fire lit under my bottom to invoke the various literary bludgeons contained in that poison pen letter was stoked by our local chief of police, a friend and former employer. He stated in an interview that the war on drugs would never be won until various changes were made in the United States Constitution. These changes would have meant less freedom for all of us, although directed at the criminal. No one despises dopers and stealers more than I. Just the same, crime drugs and pilferage are trade-offs in a free society. We may be in danger, but at least we have the right-and the means-to self defense. It is often said that the man who does not frequent rough bars or seedy sections of town and does not consort with prostitutes is relatively safe in America. This is true to an extent. But many attacks are crimes of opportunity and chance and unpredictable.

The handgun is a weapon of opportunity to combat crimes of opportunity. A rifle or shotgun is a better weapon for fighting, but the handgun is carried as a weapon of defense against unforeseen trouble. Light, portable, concealable and fast into action, the handgun is our most useful defensive firearm. A handgun is problematical in effectiveness. In skilled hands the pistol can prove lethal and effective. Sgt Alvin York is one example of this, Marshal Wyatt Earp another. In untrained hands the pistol can be as dangerous to its wielder as the adversary. I won't sugarcoat the issue. Handguns can be safely used by anyone, male or female, of normal strength and coordination. Race and national original are not impediments but temperament is. An open mind dedicated to learning is required. Quality gear is not inexpensive, proficiency at arms is purchased with a different coin.

A concealed carry handgun is part of a system that includes a good holster, support gear, and most of all the human component. Some of the system is hardware, some of it software. Most of the system comes from adaptation. Let take a hard look at the selection of the proper handgun and the life saving skills that make it effective.

CHAPTER TWO
HAND GUN TYPES

Fighting is fighting and tactics are never outdated. But weapons changed often during the past few decades. We have seen the revolver replaced as the primary police service weapon, while it still enjoys a great deal of popularity with civilians, especially when it comes to smaller concealment pieces. Autoloaders offer advantages over the revolver, most of which are based on a perceived need for more 'firepower.' Revolver shooters remind us you cannot miss fast enough to keep up and that only hits count. If you do not get your man down with the first three rounds or do not find cover, your war is probably over. Just the same, autos do offer significant advantages. Among autloaders there are differences in operation and function which we will address. In the end, we will see that some of us prefer one type over the other and should choose the handgun we use best and feel most comfortable with. The revolver is clearly the model of simplicity. Simplicity of operation in stressful situations is always an advantage. Autoloaders range from almost revolver simple to several levels of complexity. I have listed some of the obvious and subtle differences in the two types.

Consider your needs and ability carefully.

The revolver or the auto can serve, but the user must have consummate skill in application. These are two of the best - the Wilson Combat CQB .45 auto and the Smith & Wesson L frame .357 Magnum.

ADVANTAGES AND DISADVANTAGES

Semi-Auto

Seen as the more modern type

Offers more rounds, i.e. 'Firepower'

Offers some security against a gun grab attempt in those models fitted with a manual safety.

This is a double action 457 .45 auto from Smith & Wesson - the knife is an automatic from Taylor Cutlery

Due to reciprocating action and more efficient use of powder capacity, the auto recoils less than a revolver of comparable power-revolver cartridges use larger charges of comparatively slower burning powder to achieve similar results.

The auto offers better hit probability under stress.

Autoloaders are more controllable in rapid fire.

Revolver

Proven in operation

Can be stored for long periods of time with all springs at rest and can be counted on to come up firing

The double action revolver can still serve well as this well shot up reaction plate at Spartanburg City Police Club tells us

Can be placed against an opponent's body and fired repeatedly with no danger of gun jamming.

Above all else, simple to operate - you only need to aim the gun and pull the trigger.

Quality revolvers are often less expensive than quality autoloaders.

Revolvers chamber the most powerful cartridges.

Here is the manual arms of various types of handguns. The manual of arms is simply the motions needed to load, make the gun safe, and then to fire the weapon.

MANUAL OF ARMS

Revolver	Double Action Only Auto	Double Action Auto/decocker
Load	Load	Load
Holster	Holster	Decock
Draw	Draw	Holster
Fire	Fire	Draw
		Fire

Double Action Auto	Single Action Auto with safety
Load	Load
Decock	Place Safety On
Holster	Holster
Draw	Draw
Move safety to fire position	Move Safety to fire position
Fire	Fire

As you can see, some handguns have a manual of arms more complex than others. Simplicity favors the double action revolver. I have seen students begin successfully with all types of pistols, but the double action revolver is the ideal handgun for first time shooters. With its long smooth trigger, safety is there-but true safety is only between the ears of the shooter. You may visually confirm the revolver is loaded simply by opening the cylinder and observing the gun load of cartridges.

TYPES OF AUTOLOADERS

A double action trigger simply means the trigger action does two things-it both cocks the hammer and fires the gun. A double action revolver uses trigger action to cock the hammer, rotate the cylinder, and fire the gun. But most revolvers can be cocked for a crisp let off. This is referred to as single action fire. A double action semi-auto uses trigger action to cock and fire the gun. However, after the first shot, the slide recoils and cocks the hammer for subsequent single-action shots. A double action only autopistol requires a long pull of the trigger for each and every shot. As a result, they are the most difficult of all types to use well. A single action handgun requires the trigger be cocked before it is brought into action. Most single action autos are designed to be

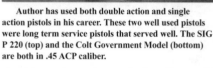

carried cocked with the safety on. Colt 1911 single action pistols are designed to be carried cocked and locked, hammer fully cocked, with the safety on. Double action pistols such as the Beretta 92 may be carried safety on or safety off with a degree of safety. The SIG P series has no manual safety, but a long

Author has used both double action and single action pistols in his career. These two well used pistols were long term service pistols that served well. The SIG P 220 (top) and the Colt Government Model (bottom) are both in .45 ACP caliber.

double action trigger SIG calls a safety 'feature'. The Glock has the same trigger action for every shot and while termed a double action only handles much like a single action with no safety. The utmost care is needed in handling this type of handgun.

The single action pistol, with only one trigger action to learn, is the easiest handgun to master in terms of trigger action. The trigger action of the single action allows a short, straight to the rear compression.

Whatever the handgun, trigger discipline is demanded. The finger must stay off the trigger until the gun is to be fired. Not when you think you will fire, but when you fire!

All handguns are a trade off of sort, and quite a few modern handguns are a triumph of the technical over the tactical. I do not care for double action only service guns.

Compact, simple, and reliable, the Glock 23 is an estimatable service handgun well-suited to personal defense

They are difficult to use well and seem more a sop to liability and administrators more interested in cutting the training budget than in saving lives. Just the same, two modern DAO designs are impressive. One is the successful Light

Double Action marketed by Para Ordnance. These .45 caliber pistols offer a clean fresh design with much merit. In compact pistols, the Kahr DAO guns are attractive, reliable, and offer an excellent trigger action.

In double action pistols, the Beretta design is the most proven. This pistol is a large and bulky gun but offers good reliability. The SIG is often more accurate, and always a good choice. The Smith and Wesson Third Generation pistols offer stainless steel construction and the finest safety system of any double action autoloading pistol. As an all around handgun, the Smith and Wesson is a good choice.

This is a new type of 1911 pistol from Para Ordnance. The Light Double Action (LDA) is gaining wide and well-deserved acceptance

In the single action pistol type, the Colt pistols have given good service. New models seem better than anything we had in the past. My personal High Standard G Man has proven a good solid handgun. The Kimber is a good choice, now used by the LAPD SWAT team. The best buy on a 1911 pistol in my opinion is the Kimber Custom II. This is a good solid pistol with many features. Traditionalists will like the styling, the modern shooter, the features. The Wilson Combat pistol is not inexpensive but is an extraordinary handgun. The 1911 is a good handgun, a weapon proven in combat. But it does not suffer fools well and demands training and regular practice. Be honest with yourself when choosing the handgun.

CHAPTER THREE
HANDGUN RELIABILITY

If you have chosen a revolver over the autoloader for reliability reasons you have done well-but a number of modern handguns are almost incredibly reliable. It has been said the revolver will take a lot of use, but autoloaders will stand more abuse. This may be true. With proper care, lubrication, and maintenance, a quality handgun will out last most users.

A Glock pistol during author's torture tests

Extreme testing by the FBI, Ohio State Patrol, LAPD, Russian Spetnatz, California Highway Patrol, and the Royal Canadian Mounties have established a number of handguns have excellent reliability, reliability being the tendency to the weapon to fire and continue to fire with each pull of the trigger. Personal favorites aside, these figures are hard to argue with. As an example, the OSP conducted a test program which expended well over two hundred thousand cartridges in one hundred seventy handguns. This test will be a paradigm for future selection. It will be difficult to support an alternate selection not based on similar tests.

Civilian gun carriers could do far worse than to choose one of the handguns chosen by these agencies. Beware copycats and doubtful configu-

A Smith & Wesson forzen in muddy, soupy water

rations which mimic these handguns. As an example, the Kimber Target II cost just over one thousand dollars. An inexpensive

9

version simply cannot possess the same attributes. The following handguns have passed strict tests with various agencies and have proven more than effective in the field.

Colt 1911	US Army Test
Beretta 92 9mm	US Army and Border Patrol test programs.
SIG P series: P 220,	
P 226, P 228 and P 229	European police trails and in America, the stringent OSP test showed the SIG P 226 to a reli able handgun.
SIG P 228	US Army trails
Glock 22 & Glock 23	FBI trails
Smith & Wesson 4006	California Highway Patrol Test
CZ 75 9mm	Various Soviet Bloc test programs
Smith & Wesson 3953, 5946	RCMP police trails
Kimber 1911	LAPD selection process, Tacoma, WA PD test
Springfield Bureau Model	FBI, SWAT testing
Revolvers	
Smith & Wesson K frame	Model Ten, Model 19
Ruger GP 100	
Ruger SP 101	

With proper maintenance most quality handguns will give many years of service. When used weekly, they will stand up to this practice regimen and remain ready when needed.   Other, less expensive handguns can lay at wait under the counter or in the home for years and perform when needed. But only by carefully testing these handguns will you arrive at the proper choice for you. There are quite a few disastrous handguns marketed, weapons that are hard to use well and less than reliable. You will not see them in this book.

CHAPTER FOUR
WOUND POTENTIAL

Some say a firearm is only a projectile launcher and no better than its projectiles. There is much truth in this statement. Compared to a shotgun or a centerfire rifle, the handgun is a weak instrument. The 'strong .45' and 'weak .38' are more alike than they differ when matched against a 12 gauge

High velocity bullets produce interesting results, but a splash of water, while dramatic, does not tell us much

shotgun or a .30 caliber rifle. But within their range, with proper ammunition, they can serve adequately in the personal defense role. Handgun cartridges do not have 'stopping power,' vehicle brakes have stopping power. Cartridges do have wound potential. This is simply the ability of the projectile to create damage in bone, muscle and tissue. The single most important aspect of wound potential is penetration. The bullet must reach vital organs. The bullet should also be of sufficient diameter to create a large wound. The only reliable mechanism of collapse in a human subject is blood loss. The only reliable predictor of cartridge effectiveness is a test program which measures the depth of penetration and bullet expansion. Large caliber bullets have an advantage in that they destroy more tissue and create a larger wound channel. Until the laws of physics are changed this will always be the case.

So, then, why don't we all carry .44 Magnum revolvers? A balance between power and controllability is needed. A balance of expansion and penetration is also needed, whatever the caliber. Too little penetration or too much expansion and the bullet stops short of vital blood bearing organs. A superficial wound is the result. Calibers below .38 Special +P cannot be counted upon to provide both expansion and penetration. The Federal Bureau of Investigation has performed extensive testing of handgun cartridges and established wound values for various calibers and load combinations. At this point, someone will mention the various 'studies' and 'tests' of handguns and ammunition. I can only state that a scientist allows others to observe his tests and supplies empirical data. The true test of science is that it be verifiable and repeatable.

Anonymous tests meet none of this criteria. As Sgt. Chris Pollack observed in the pages of Law and Order, to believe in some such data is to believe in Little Green Men. We do not believe in Little Green Men.

Some have proclaimed that the FBI results over-stressed penetration. The FBI

Service handgun cartridges must meet strict criteria including vehicle glass penetration

understands the problem better than most of us, and has tremendous resources. They also have hundreds of knowledgeable agents who are interested in firearms. They understood that most FBI agents engaged in gunfire encountered felons behind vehicles. Thirteen of the last seventeen police shooting histories I collected involved felons in vehicles. I have no secret sources, I simply follow-up initial reports found in newspapers or television reports. Consider the problem. If a felon is firing at you, he will probably be standing erect and holding the weapon in front of his body. The arms will be locked together in a two hand load, or perhaps he will hold the handgun in one hand at full extension. Your bullet may have to penetrate the heavy bones of his arms and retain sufficient penetration to penetrate the chest and engage blood bearing organs. If the opponent is heavily clad, especially if he is wearing a leather jacket, the chances of certain bullets reaching the necessary depth of penetration is slim. Even worse, if the felon is behind a vehicle glass or other light cover, the chances of the projectile having good effect may be slim.

It is true that civilian scenarios seldom call for such penetration. Special loadings are offered which are labeled 'Personal Defense' loads. These are tailored for defensive scenarios. As might be expected, the weaker the caliber the more important load selection is. But I would not agonize over the choice. Choose a high quality brand with good design features and concentrate on marksmanship. The difference in a shot to the intestines and a blow to the heart is the real difference in loads. Accuracy can make up for power, the reverse is seldom true. Or, as former Detroit homicide officer Evan Marshall told us, there are three main components of 'stopping power.' Marksmanship. Marksmanship. Marksmanship.

However, what must not be ignored is reliability and cartridge integrity. I have conducted ammunition test programs for police agencies over the years, and quite a few loadings did not make the grade. We validated reliability before considering ballistic effect. First, I soaked cartridges in water overnight to see if they fired after this immersion. Most passed. Those that did not pass showed poor case mouth seal-we never had a primer failure, but experienced several powder failures. Re-manufactured ammunition does not have effective case mouth and primer seal in comparison to factory new ammunition, but you are warned before the purchase. A number of generic brands also cut case mouth seal as a cost saving measure. However, low cost is not always a badge of inferior quality. As an example, remanufactured loadings from 3 D Ammunition, a subsidiary of Hornady Custom Ammunition, were used as controls. None failed the initial test, due largely to efficient manufacture and excellent quality control.

After the initial water tests other examples of ammunition were exposed to solvent and left immersed overnight. The failure rate changed little. Next, since we were testing semi auto ammunition, we tested the case mouth and crimp seal. I chambered the same cartridge as many as twenty times in various pistols. An officer or armed civilian unloading his gun for safe keeping or inspection follows several regimens. He normally unloads the gun, then replaces the round removed from the chamber in the magazine of his pistol, and reloads the gun. In a month the same cartridge can be rechambered up to thirty times. We cannot expect a cartridge to survive unlimited chambering but when the bullet is forced into the case by a measurable degree in a half dozen chamberings,

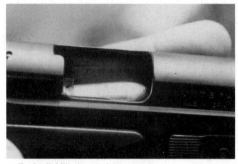

Feed reliability is most important

this load is hardly suitable for police service. Few interested in personal defense perform these simple tests. They can be life-savers.

A full powder burn is a desirable trait I find more common among police cartridges. Not long ago my agency qualified with Winchester USA ball ammunition, the least expensive factory ammunition we could find. After firing over two hundred rounds in qualification, my SIG had a few unburned powder kernels and little other evidence of powder ash. All of the powder was burning in the handgun's barrel. Low muzzle flash is a product of a full powder burn. Bright muzzle flash is to be avoided. Many handgun actions take place in dim light. A bright flash can be disconcerting.

Few if any foreign concerns produce ammunition even roughly comparable to American offerings. That is the reason companies such as Speer and Federal are successful in marketing ammunition in Europe. A sole exception in my experience is the GECO Blunt Action Trauma round, but this load is no longer available in America. In any case there are loads equally effective available domestically. I have tested various specialty loads from Hirtenberger and Lapua in 9mm Luger caliber, and while accuracy and quality was good overall performance, especially in terms of expansion, was lacking.

Beware generic equivalent loads. By that I mean do not listen to the man who tells you that all loads are the same, and the various makers, foreign and domestic, have the loadings down pat and that all are the same. This can lead to tragic mistakes. I personally favor 115 grain jacketed hollowpoint loadings in the 9mm Luger caliber, but I am aware that the deviation in penetration and expansion of all loads is near one hundred per cent! As retold in Second Chance Vest, Incorporated's video, *Second Chance Versus The Cop Killers*, a western agency made a terrible mistake in buying cartridges on the low bid.

This is a perfectly expanded Gold Dot bullet

They performed a test which concluded the 115 grain 9mm load was the ideal performer, but then ordered a foreign brand on the low bid. In a shooting event, a felon absorbed seventeen hits, finally being stopped by a cranio ocular strike. Non expanding bullets produce a narrow, needle like profile. The underdeveloped hollowpoint loaded in this cartridge was not roughly comparable to our own Hydra Shock, SXT, Silvertip, or XTP bullet-but it was less expensive. All loadings are not the same! Take care in ammunition selection. Above all else, the ammunition must be reliable.

Quality generic or remanufactured ammunition can be used for practice, but we must allocate the funds necessary to fully test our handgun with the chosen defense loading. A minimum of one hundred trouble free rounds is one standard, but my personal standards are more demanding. You will find that quality ammunition and quality handguns are very reliable indeed.

As for ballistic performance, a minium of ten inches of penetration is needed for adequate performance in all scenarios. Expansion of jacketed hollowpoint bullets will be reliable in test media such as wet newsprint and ballistic gelatin, but just the same medical examiners and the FBI report that perhaps one half to three quarters of all jacketed hollowpoint bullets that meet flesh blood and bone expand as designed. Ammunition and caliber choice are important, but in the end shot placement matters the most.

GELATIN RESULTS POPULAR LOADS & CALIBERS

Penetration is measured in depth, expansion is the widest point of the average of recovered bullets.

*Recommended load

Caliber	Load	Velocity	Penetration	Expansion
.380 ACP	WW 96 gr. SXT	887 fps	9 in.	.55
.380 ACP	Black Hills 90 gr.JHP	974 fps	11.5in.	.52
All .38 Special results are from 2 inch barrel handguns				
.38 Special	WW 110 gr. Silvertip	807 fps	6.4in.	.53
*.38 Special	WW 158 gr. LSWCHP	774 fps	13.5in.	.54
.38 Special	Federal 129gr. Hydra Shock	890 fps	9.9 in.	.56
.357 Magnum	WW 110 gr. JHP	1299 fps	10 in.	.56
*.357 Magnum	WW 125 gr. JHP	1367 fps	12.5in.	.65
*.357 Magnum	WW 145 gr. Silvertip	1329 fps	14 in.	.80
.357 SIG	Federal 125 gr. JHP	1352 fps	14.5 in.	.68
.357 SIG	Cor Bon 115 gr. JHP	1509 fps	9in.	.55
The above load fragmented, leaving a .55 caliber core.				
9mm Luger	Cor Bon 90 gr. JHP	1515 fps	5 in.	.60
Fragmented				
9mm Luger	WW 115 gr. +P+	1307 fps	8 in.	.80
9mm Luger	WW 115 gr. Silvertip	1180 fps	8 in.	.68

Caliber	Load	Velocity	Penetration	Expansion
*9mm Luger	Black Hills 115 gr. +P	1304 fps	11 in.	.59
*9mm Luger	Hornady 124 grain JHP	1170 fps	12in.	.64
9mm Luger	WW 147 gr. SXT	1004 fps	14 in.	.51
.40 S & W	Cor Bon 135 gr. JHP	1291 fps	9 in.	.55
*.40 S&W	Federal 155 gr. Hydra Shock	1140 fps	13in.	.69
*.40 S & W	W W 155 gr. Silvertip	1175 fps	12.2in.	.76
*.44 Special	Cor Bon 165 gr. JHP	930 fps	10in.	.70
.45 ACP	Federal 165 gr. PD*	1038 fps	10in.	.74

PD is the abbreviation of Personal Defense

Caliber	Load	Velocity	Penetration	Expansion
*.45 ACP	Remington185 gr.JHP	1001 fps	12 in.	.87
*.45 ACP	Remington185gr.JHP+P	1122 fps	11 in.	.55*

Fragmented

Caliber	Load	Velocity	Penetration	Expansion
*.45 ACP	Hornady 230 gr XTP	909 fps	13.5 in.	.68
*.45 ACP	Federal 230gr. Hydra Shock	855 fps	12 in.	.70
*.45 ACP	Black Hills 230 gr. JHP	898 fps	14. in.	.70
*.45 ACP	Cor Bon 230 gr. JHP	915 fps	12.1in.	.74

CHAPTER FIVE
HANDGUN CARTRIDGES

In the previous chapter we discussed wound ballistics and performance. It may seem redundant, but at this point it behooves us to examine the various handgun cartridges. Some are quite popular and a number of others are specialist's cartridges. In the wound ballistics chapter, we had hard science to guide us. Some of the choices in cartridges are more subjective. But they are grounded in fact. Take your counsel but when possible, err on the side of caution.

The .45 acp remains one of the few cartridges that is effective without an expanding bullet. A hit to the body may disable a felon without killing him, not true if he is hit by five or six small bore cartridges in an attempt to stop him. This is 1,000 rounds of .45 ACP Remington hardball.

HANDGUN CALIBERS
.22 Long Rifle

Often touted as the ideal cartridge for a beginner, this is the finest practice and informal target cartridge available. Inexpensive and accurate, the .22 Long Rifle has been pressed into service as a defense cartridge. It meets one requirement for a defense cartridge-penetration. Properly delivered, it will serve but not well. Any cartridge will kill, but lethality is irrelevant. We wish to stop the adversary. The stopping of an adversary can often be accomplished without killing him if a big bore bullet is delivered to major bones, but a body riddled with small caliber holes will not live long. Conversely, you cannot shoot an adversary a little bit. The .22 is fine for practice.

.25 ACP

The .25 ACP is a centerfire cartridge. As such it is far more resistant to oil, solvent and rough handling than the .22 Long Rifle. It's jacketed bullet is far less likely to be damaged than the heel based lead bullet of the .22 Long Rifle. However, the .25 ACP seems considerably less effective than the .22 in my perception. The roundnose bullet tends to bounce off bone, even skull bone. I have in my data base a number of very poor results with the .25. On the other hand, I have two in which the .25 performed beyond all expectation, with five chest hits stopping a car-jacker and a single hit in another case stopping an angry 250 pound man in his tracks. This man required extensive surgery and seven weeks in the hospital. No one wants to get shot, and the little guns are deterrents. The best use I have seen of the .25 is when a homeowner fired a single round into his garage and a burglar leapt through a window frame to get away. Most .25 ACP pistols are of poor construction, unreliable, and unsafe. A striker fired autoloader that requires two hands to get into action is best used as a fishing weight.

.32 ACP

I have shot the Savage .32, the Colt 1903, and the SAUER 38 H often in this caliber. In modern handguns, I have extensive experience with the Kel Tec K 32. It is reliable and easy to use well, a good anti mugger piece. It is safe to carry fully loaded and remains the sole excuse for carrying a .32 caliber pistol. The .32 ACP is little better than the .25 ACP, but can be accurate in quality weapons. Keep in mind that the .32 ACP generates 1,000 fps with the 71 grain load in this caliber, when fired in the Colt 1903. Most pocket revolvers in .32 and .38 Smith and Wesson only generated 600-680 fps, providing poor penetration. If you must carry a small handgun, the .32 ACP is quite accurate and some handguns are reliable. Multiple strikes to the torso are the only chance with this one.

.380 ACP

Most .32 ACP pistols can also be had in .380 ACP. As such, the larger caliber is the better choice. Some very well made, reliable handguns are chambered for this cartridge. However, I have noted very poor results with this caliber. A local judge saved his life simply by holding his hand in front of his face, stopping a .380 ACP bullet! Some authorities feel the .32 ACP is more feed reliable and more accurate than the .380. I have seen little to choose between them. These cartridges are little more effective, in the real world, than the .22 and are best avoided. A quality 9mm Luger caliber compact pistol is larger but about as easy to use well. The main value of the small calibers is in deterrent.

9 x 18 Makarov

The 9 x 18 Makarov is slightly more powerful than the .380 ACP, moving a heavier bullet as much as 100 fps faster than the .380. In full metal jacket form, it is probably as good a short range defense caliber as any other 9mm/.38. The Hornady loading is accurate and offers a degree of expansion. The Makarov pistol is a military design and as such very reliable. It is affordable, which is not always true of compact 9mm caliber pistols. And, while we like to praise compact 9mm pistols, the need to operate the pistol safely with high pressure ammunition dictates locked breech operation. The 9 x 18 operates with a blow back principle. In other words, the Makarov, PPK, SIG P 230 and others have a fixed barrel. The slide recoils from the barrel. A locked breech handgun uses a system in which the slide and barrel recoil in a unit. As a result, the blow back pistol is simpler and more compact. The Makarov can be purchased for half the price of a quality 9mm, but it is reliable and accurate. But the cartridge is not enough, and there is the quandary. The man or woman on a budget is well served with the Makarov and Hornady ammunition, within the limits of the caliber.

.38 Special

I don't like to quote figures which place cartridge effectiveness in neat little boxes.

Among the few studies I lend some credence to is the Police Marksmans Association Study. The sources were open to all, and the figures seem realistic, per my research. The standard velocity non expanding .38 Special roundnose lead bullet proved capable of stopping felons with a single shot an average of one time in four. In common parlance, it was about twenty five per cent effective. The standard velocity .38 has nothing to recommend it.

.38 Special +P

This is first caliber we have discussed that may be considered a reliable personal defense cartridge. Indeed, some experts such as David W. Arnold feel this is the largest caliber the average shooter can handle well. It requires much practice and more than a little expense to produce an honest advantage over the .38 Special +P. But only a few loads are proven in the defense field, many others seem promising but do not always perform well. When conditions are good for expansion, and this relies a great deal upon shot placement, the 125 grain jacketed hollowpoints work well. But the best loading for the .38 Special is the 158 grain lead semi wadcutter hollowpoint. This is basically a legitimized handload. For many years the Keith style hollowpoint was recommended to handloaders for use in the .38. With it's soft lead construction this bullet has a far lower expansion threshold than any jacketed bullet. In other words, it will begin expansion at a lower velocity than jacketed bullets. There is some evidence this bullet expands even more the harder resistance it meets. In other words, a large heavily muscled individual will cause the bullet to expand more than a small lightly clad individual would. I once worked with an agency that issued this load and no other. Results were good. The load has seen much use in snub nose or two inch barrel revolvers. It seems to maintain a degree of authority despite some velocity loss in these compact revolvers. I have seen the 110 grain JHP flatten out on a skull, only producing stunning effect. The Winchester 158 grain SWC HP, also known as the FBI load due to the Bureau's adoption of this load, has an excellent balance of expansion and penetration. The .38 +P is a fine cartridge, one of the best choices available in personal defense.

.357 Magnum

This cartridge is often hailed as the best manstopper of all time. I cannot argue with this consensus. When a cop tells you he saw a gunfight or a knife fight, what he means is 'I arrived just as the fight was over.' Peace officers who have been in service for long periods, especially in places like Area Six, Chicago, or Forth Apache, New York, have seen the aftermath of numerous gun battles. I have seen the effect of the .357 Magnum over the top of my own gunsights. Based purely on terminal performance, the .357 Magnum is the single most effective handgun cartridge. The need for a second shot, given good placement of the initial shot, is a rarity. However, this is a true Magnum loading that is hard on both the gun and the shooter.

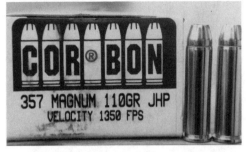

The good old 'Magnum' is still a fine cartridge with much to recommend it.

Control is difficult and the load can produce flinching. The cartridge should never be used in handguns with barrels below four inches in length. In short barrels the relatively slow burning powders used in the Magnum are not optimized and much of the performance of the caliber is lost. The ideal Magnum is a medium frame revolver such as the Ruger GP 100 or Smith and Wesson L Frame. I like the K Combat Magnum when fitted with recoil absorbing Hogue grips. Avoid Magnums with ported barrels. Not only is muzzle blast ear splitting but velocity is robbed terribly, putting the Magnum in .38 Special class. The Magnum is well worth mastering but it is no weekend task.

.357 SIG

The .357 SIG is a .40 caliber Smith and Wesson necked down to 9mm. The round jolts a 125 grain Jacketed Hollow Point to well over 1350 fps. The Cor Bon 115 grain JHP breaks 1,500 fps from a Glock 4.49 inch barrel, somewhat less from a SIG. I have fired this round extensively in a Bar Sto barreled Glock with excellent results and good accuracy. This cartridge is intended to bring .357 Magnum ballistics to the semi auto. It does just that. Of course it does not equal the Magnum's performance with heavy 140 to 180 grain bullets, the .357 SIG can use no bullet heavier than 147 grains and is at it's best with 124 grain bullets. But it does in fact equal four inch barrel .357 Magnum revolver ballistics. I conducted a test for Police Magazine involving a number of pistol cartridges, and the .357 SIG produced the best vehicle penetration of any cartridge. It is promising. For pure personal defense, I prefer the .40 caliber, but with the Cor Bon loading the .357 SIG should be dynamite for personal defense. The average law enforcement load does not have the dynamic expansion of the .357 Magnum bullets, and is on the long end of expansion. If you have a need for outstanding penetration, this is the caliber.

9mm Luger

Of all the cartridges I have tested, the 9mm Luger runs the highest deviation in performance. As an example, when testing handgun cartridges for a southern department, penetration tests showed a

Modern powder technology has pushed the 9mm Luger to the low end limits of the .33 Magnum in velocity

one hundred per cent deviation in this caliber, with jacketed hollowpoint bullets penetrating five to eighteen inches of gelatin, a greater range than any other caliber. With non expanding ammunition, this caliber is no more effective than the .38 Special. With properly designed jacketed hollowpoint bullets the 9mm Luger, by virtue of relatively high velocity, can promote upset of JHP bullets reliably. I prefer the 115 grain JHP, with the 124 grain JHP a better choice when intermediate objects are a concern. The 9mm Luger is not as weak as its detractors claim but neither is it as good as its proponents would like us to believe. It is a reasonable choice for personal defense. Due to the relatively fast burning powders used in the 9mm Luger, and the recoiling action of the autoloader, the 9mm produces less recoil given loads of similar power than any .38 caliber revolver. With top end loads, the 9mm outstrips the .38 Special in paper ballistics. In the real world, each is similar in effectiveness and very load specific in effectiveness.

.38 ACP Super

An elegant old cartridge chambered in the 1911 style pistols and the SIG P 220. If for some reason an individual cannot handle the recoil of the .45 the .38 Super is an alternative. The .38 Super is offered in .45 frame handguns. The .900 inch long case of the Super limits the cartridge to these full size handguns. I am unaware of a single shooting with the .38 Super in my experience. Therefore, a professional opinion and declaration is difficult. I have shot animals of various types with the Super, and it seems in the .357 Magnum class, at least with common loads in four inch barrel revolvers. Cor Bon loadings put this cartridge squarely in the .357 SIG class.

.40 Smith and Wesson

This caliber has taken the police market by storm. It is not as popular with civilians and the bad guys, who once were on the .40 caliber bandwagon, now seem to cling to their '9s'. The .40 is a fine cartridge. It offers big bore performance on a 9mm frame. Its short case allows chambering in compact, handy firearms. The .40 is more difficult to control than the 9mm Luger and may

intimidate some shooters. For my use, if I want more shots I use a 9mm, if I want knockdown power, I use the .45. But the .40 is here to stay. The 165 grain Black Hills JHP is easily the most accurate single

Primer seal and placement is perfect in these rounds of .400-Cor Bon

loading I have tested. Others, such as the Winchester Silvertip, offer ideal ballistic performance. Loads in the 150 to 165 grain range give excellent results. I have taken a whitetail deer with this caliber. With a single neck hit it was four legs in the air, instantly. This cartridge is one of the best personal defense choices. Coupled with a quality compact handgun such as the Kahr K 40, you are as well armed as you can be with a concealable lightweight pistol.

10mm Auto

The 10mm is seldom seen in civilian holsters, but it is an interesting cartridge. Every 10mm pistol I have tested has been accurate and reliable. With Cor Bon ammunition, my personal Glock 20 has placed five rounds in less than an inch at twenty five yards, uncanny performance. The 10mm is another long case cartridge suitable only for .45 caliber frame pistols.

The 10mm is available in two power levels. The first is in the .40 Smith and Wesson class and very controllable in full size pistols. The second power level is in the .357 Magnum class.

If I were carrying this caliber for personal defense, I would seriously consider the Hornady 155 grain XTP loading. This is a special purpose caliber. I have come to prefer the .45 +P if I need more power in an autopistol. There are not enough 10mm cases on record to give a good understanding of the cartridge's ability. Many of the early shootings occurred with hard jacketed foreign ammunition, giving the 10mm a black eye that may of been undeserved. Like the .38 Super, this one is carried on faith and scientific test results. That is not enough for the pragmatic observer. I do have one case in which a female cop shot an armed felon. The shot went through the car windshield and the single chest hit immediately stopped the felon. The load was the Pro Load 180 grain, which used the 180 grain Gold Dot bullet. The medical examiner told me that if he had the felon on an operating table a second after the shot, he could not have saved him. By the same token, had the officer fired a second later her life could well of been over. I believe the 10mm, with proper loads and in good hands, can do the business.

When we move to the big bore revolver cartridges, we find cartridges that can only be chambered in relatively heavy, bulky revolvers. These guns are much slower to bring into action than a conventional mid frame .357 Magnum revolver. Some shooters feel comfortable with these cartridges, and they are good choices. To each his own.

.41 Magnum

A good cartridge. It is more powerful than the 10mm auto by

a margin, and more controllable than the .44 Magnum revolver. The Winchester Silvertip is the only reasonable choice for self defense. In the Smith and Wesson Model 57 a gilt edged accurate combination. I have heard good things about the Taurus Tracker revolver, from reliable sources.

.44 Special

I have recorded mixed results with the .44 Special. With roundnose lead bullets this caliber is no more effective than the .38 Special. Due to the low velocities involved with this caliber, bullet expansion with jacketed hollowpoint bullets is seldom good. I would load the CCI Gold Dot 200 grain JHP or the Cor Bon 165 grain JHP load and hope for the best.

.44 Magnum

With the possible exception of the 10mm auto and the .41 Magnum, this is the first cartridge discussed that need not rely upon bullet expansion for effectiveness. The .44 cuts a deep wide wound channel without JHP bullets. . I have used the .44 on game up to 280 pounds with excellent results. Every case I have on hand shows a one shot stop. In one case, a single shot to the knee dropped an assailant immediately. The .44 Magnum exhibits severe recoil. It kicks approximately four times as hard as the .45 ACP. There is a real danger of over-penetration. In one incident in my jurisdiction, a homeowner fired his .44 Magnum once at an adversary. The bullet struck the man in the liver and immediately destroyed this solid organ. The man fell to the floor and died. However, the bullet exited and struck the shooter's wife in the shoulder, crippling her. The .44 Magnum is not too much for personal defense, Dirty Harry aside. The best choice in a carry load is the Winchester Silvertip, a reduced power load with plenty of energy.

If defense against large animals is a consideration, the .44 Magnum is a good choice. The big Magnum requires practice and dedication to master.

.45 Colt

The .45 Colt is used more now than ever before. Many shooters are enjoying Cowboy Action and keep their .45s by the bedside. The .45 will serve, and serve well, but it is not among the more efficient calibers. The case was designed for bulky black powder, not modern smokeless powder. Factory lead hollowpoints or the Silvertip load break just over 750 fps. I have seen a 225 grain lead SWCHP stopped in the vinyl trim of a car door. Even worse, the .45 Colt case rim is too small for efficient use with modern star ejecting double action revolvers. It is at its best in button ejecting single action revolvers. At this time the best factory loads are the original 255 grain conical loads as loaded by Remington and Winchester. An alternative is to special order the Cor Bon JHP load, which gives far better ballistic performance than any I am aware of. Those are the big bore revolver cartridges.

.45 ACP

The .45 ACP is the most efficient handgun cartridge for personal defense, and it is available in both pistols and revolvers. The cartridge has good accuracy potential, usually shows a full powder burn, and is well balanced. The cartridge does not rely upon bullet expansion for effectiveness but rather on frontal area and bullet mass. The .45 has penetration, bullet diameter, and bullet weight. The guns that chamber the .45 ACP can be used well and quickly. Recoil is certainly greater than experienced with the 9mm Luger or .40 S & W, but not nearly the problem to control the Magnum revolvers are. The .45 does demand a regular commitment to practice.

That sums up the readily available handgun cartridges. There are many trick loadings that attempt to alter the performance of a cartridge. Some loads allow medium game to be taken with a handgun. As an example, the Cor Bon 180 grain bonded core load turns the .357 Magnum into a quite effective deer load. But the basic power of a caliber-physics, remember?-cannot be changed. Only how that power is applied or used is open to change. Expanding bullets benefit the medium calibers most. The .38 Special and 9mm Luger are vastly improved by the integration of expanding bullets into the load. The small calibers do not have adequate power to properly utilize expanding bullets, and the larger calibers are effective without expanding bullets. The most important component the equation is still the man or woman behind the gun.

Chapter Six
The Shooter - Cornerstones of Proficiency

The shooter is the brain of this system and the most important part of any self defense plan. What is in his brain and in muscle memory will carry the day. When the ball goes up for real, you will not rise to the occasion. You will revert to trained response at a predictably lower level than you have reached in training. Training by repetition is vital. If you can afford the time and money to do so, attend a reputable shooting school. I recommend you contact The Lethal Force Institute. You will find contact information for several

This shooter is firing using the proven Weaver stance, but in a modified version without a sharp slant in the weak arm

schools in the index. I have seen numerous horrendous ideas taught by those who should know better, at the expense of their students. At last count, one state agency had paid out millions in lawsuits, and I know the source of most of the trouble. I will state for the record that America exports experts of all types, military and police, worldwide. American military and police training is the envy of the world. While I welcome refugees from various monarchies and People's Republics, the best trainers and the best schools in the world are right here in the USA. If American training is good enough for the King of Jordan it should suit anyone, meaning he could afford anything he needed.

I have seen numerous Israeli style tactics described which left me wondering what the point was. No school that teaches chamber empty carry of a semi auto handgun should be considered. No weapon needing two hands to make ready is acceptable. If you are afraid of autopistols, carry a revolver. Again, for the American streets, American instructors.

SWAT Magazine is an objective and frank magazine. They regularly offer reviews of various schools and courses, and are an excellent resource for training information. Most of us will self train.

The cornerstones of handgun marksmanship must be understood. Most handgun fights take place at conversation distance. Marksmanship cannot be minimized, as the handgun is a difficult instrument to master. Even at a range of twenty feet the handgun must be properly indexed in order to place a hit where it will do the most good. A large target at close range is a difficult one when speed is part of the equation. Attention to the basics and constant practice will give us the edge needed to survive.

THE BASICS

The Stance

We should always begin in a kind of martial arts 'horse stance'. The body should be balanced with weight slightly forward on the weak side foot. The feet will be apart for balance but not excessively. The handgun will be presented forward in a two hand grip. Only at very short range, in severe conditions, should be handgun be fired with only one hand supporting the weapon.

This is the horse stance

Noted trainer and writer Gila Hayes shows how it is done with the Glock

The Grip

I use the competitors grip. Sixty per cent of the pressure is

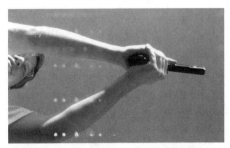

This is a view of the Weaver showing components

in the support hand. This keeps the firing hand from being tired and aids fine motor movements such as squeezing a trigger. I lock both my thumbs forward. When the thumbs lock, the other eight digits lock in unison. This is an aid in stable shooting and controlling handguns. The fingers wrap around the grip and keep the weapon properly in a muzzle up attitude.

Sight Alignment

This is the lining up of the front post or sight and the rear sights. There should be an equal amount of light on each side of the front sight and the front post perfectly aligned with the tops of the rear sight.

Sight Picture

This is the superimposition of the sights on the target.

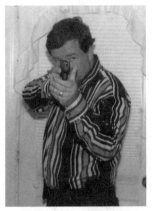

The author locked into the Weaver at close range

The sights should be centered on the target or on the leading edge of a moving target. In extreme conditions, at very close range, only the front sight may be used. In this case, the front sight should be held considerably lower than the desired point of impact.

Trigger Compression

This is the crux of marksmanship. Trigger control is everything. If the sight picture is a little off, you may still hit the target. If you jerk the trigger you will be leagues away from your mark. The trigger must be compressed straight to the rear, evenly, with every shot. The trigger must be released in order for the trigger action to reset and the trigger pressed again. A light smooth trigger helps to an extent, but a novice will clutch a too light trigger. Technique is everything. Only hundreds of repetitions of dry fire practice will produce good trigger control, coupled with live fire range drills. An important rule, firing and releasing the trigger should be equal motions for real speed.

A proper grip with a Kel Tec .32

Follow-through is difficult as well but is simple-maintain control of the weapon. When the gun fires, do not loosen your grip. This is vital to insure the bullet finds its mark, as the gun recoils while the bullet is still in the barrel. Also, we must be ready for a second shot. Followthrough is more than a function of the grip, it is a mental exercise.

Trigger compression, sight picture, the grip, followthough and proper stance will carry the day. All must be properly executed. There are two common types of two hand holds, and these are the Weaver and the Isosceles. The Isosceles is rather simple, merely thrusting the hands in front of you. The Weaver demands that the gun be drawn close and the weak arm is bent slightly in a shock absorber effect. The body is also quartered or bladed toward the target. The Weaver is a good stance, and the one I was trained on. I realize it is not friendly to movement and harder to learn than the Isosceles but my sons and I assume the Weaver in an instant, as do many other practiced shooters. To each his own. With the proper attention to basics, either will serve. Without the basics nothing will help you.

At this point, before proceeding to advanced skills, we should examine the safety aspects of a handgun. I have always thought a handgun fell somewhere between a chainsaw and a cell phone in safety requirements, and adherence to these safety rules will carry the day.

1   All guns are always loaded.
2   Never allow the gun to point at anything you do not wish to destroy. (An advanced term-Muzzle Discipline)
3   Keep your finger off the trigger until you fire. Not until you think you will fire but when you fire. (An advanced term-Trigger Discipline.)
4   Know your target, have a backstop that will contain the bullet you are using with a generous safety margin.

It is amazing how many shooters would run from a match or knife mishandled but tolerate poor gun handling. Why? They have been burnt and cut but not shot!

CHAPTER SEVEN
MAINTAINING PROFICIENCY

When we train, we train to master the basics. It is difficult to set up a scenario that will adequately train anyone for self defense problems. I can train anyone to ace the various state mandated qualifications for peace officers and armed civilians, but these are basically a bureaucratic exercise. There will be no rules, no time limits on the street. The Devil will roar like a Lion and you will be the fat in the fire. The best practice to maintain skill is to vary the regimen, working with increasingly difficult problems. In the beginning, smoothness is what will matter. Fumbles and missteps will be common. After hundreds of repetitions speed will spring from smoothness. The handgun should come to be a natural extension of your hand. I will give you an example-peace officers use their radio dozens of times a day, and reach for the microphone almost instinctively. After a few hundred repetitions

of the draw stroke you will do the same with the handgun.

Among the better steps we can take is to engage in dry fire practice. The handgun must be double checked to be certain it is unloaded. I use dry fire snap caps and

Students are often short in manipulatory skills, but these can be learned at home

dummy ammunition in my practice. These caps last forever, are brightly marked, and are an inexpensive investment in safety.

In dry fire practice, I normally draw from the holster and engage a target. I do not always fire, just as often I hold my fire. I do not wish to become a robot programmed to fire when I draw the gun. I draw and cover the target, sometimes I fire, but it is a conscious decision.

I practice the trigger stroke on the order of twenty five at a time, then rest and consider my performance. The ability to call shots, to realize whether a shot would have struck the target or not, is a good one to develop. The goal is ten perfect trigger presses per session. I do not make great claims for accuracy during initial practice sessions, but if the trigger is pressed properly and the sights are aligned, the bullet will always hit the target. There will be no excuse for a miss. A few thousand draw strokes and trigger presses will really groove you in on your handgun.

Practicing malfunction drills is important and can be addressed with dry fire, again with dummy rounds. Speed loading and using speed loaders for the various handgun types is best addressed with the triple checked unloaded handgun before

Author visualizes a target and engages in dry fire with his air weight .38

moving to live fire at the range. In all practice drills, whatever the problem to be solved, I always use sights. Anyone who recommends unsighted fire is doing the new shooter a grave disservice. Let me sum it up: I would not be the instructor who has to tell a judge,

"I taught my students not to use their sights."

Try 'instinctive driving' or 'point driving sometimes'. No, don't, that was a healthy dose of sarcasm. Use your sights at all times.

THE HOT RANGE

Now we move to the range and live fire. I do the same drills, but with loaded weapons. I draw and fire a single round, usually beginning at seven yards. Seven yards is the proverbial average distance for a gunfight, practically conversational range. By drawing and firing a single shot smoothly and eventually quickly, you will learn to address the most common scenario. A rule is that if all the shots are well centered you are going too slow and if they are scattered you are going too fast. Look at the sights, not the bullets that are striking the target. After a gunload is fired, examine the target. Establish a personal best and strive to exceed that personal best with each range trip. The target can be moved to ten yards at a later date as your skill increases.

Add an interesting dimension to practice. Don't be bored!

Do not succumb to area aiming. This is common, and must be avoided. Area aiming is aiming at the whole target. A silhouette is a pretty big target, but only a small area registers a vital hit. Aim for a specific area. If you get into trouble later with a large, heavily clad opponent and have a failure to stop problem, you will appreciate accuracy. Aim for a vital region and continue to place your shots accordingly. Once you are placing the gunload on the target, you might move up to firing two rounds on the target in cadence. This will teach recoil control and follow-through will be emphasized. I fire at five yards for this practice and move to seven yards. The rule is, fire and as soon as the sights are recovered fire again. A coarser sight picture is allowed at five yards but the longer the range the more perfect recovery must be. You will soon learn you cannot 'hose' a target and expect good results, but you will be very smooth and very fast in making multiple hits on a target. Multiple shots feel different, and you will find different problems in trigger control and sight alignment. Multiple shots are good for practice.

<u>MULTIPLE TARGETS</u>

Multiple adversaries are a daunting proposition, but with a bit of training you will be able to address these threats efficiently. Again, the best training for this type of scenario is IDPA competition and I encourage everyone to participate. Two targets about three feet apart is a good rule. You will find that you will be best served by addressing the target on the strong or gun side first then moving to the other target-it is more difficult to move in the reverse fashion. Simply draw as if engaging a single target then smoothly move to the next. Don't abruptly jerk the gun to a stop, make each movement smooth. I have found most students enjoy multiple target shooting and it gives them a degree of confidence in their handgun. The marksmanship problem is not severe as long as the student keeps his head and pays attention to the task at hand.

An important predictor of gunfight survival is whether or not the intended victim takes cover. If cover is found, the chances of survival go up quickly. IDPA matches stress cover and you should do the same in your personal regi-

Author practices trigger break in a tight situation against the wall and thereby adds this skill to muscle memory

men. It is not difficult to set up some form of cover at the range. The old police type barricade is as good as any. Firing off cover will be a discovery process. If you fire from left cover and you are right handed, the semi auto will eject cases to the right. In the opposite scenario, the gun will eject toward your cover and you may find a case bounced back and jams the gun. It happens in training and could happen for real. Malfunction drills are then executed.

I am often asked how much practice is needed. An hour a week, using fifty rounds of ammunition, is a good start. After time and as proficiency builds, you will reach a plateau at which each increment of improvement is smaller. You will find that you will retain a greater degree of skill with less practice. This takes years, and even then a modicum of practice is required to keep defense skills. For those of us who do not find adequate acceptable, constant practice is the goal. In the end, this is an investment that can pay off in high dividend.

CHAPTER EIGHT
DRILLS

In combat anything that can go wrong will, but with the solid substance of experience and drills behind you, the odds are in your favor. A few simple drills will allow you to handle most situations. Let me repeat-the basics will carry the day. But a number of drills have been established that are an aid in maintaining skill.

DRAW OR PRESENTATION FROM THE HOLSTER

Situational awareness goes a long way in avoiding critical incidents. Peace officers have developed the special sixth sense or X Ray vision that allows the individual to 'smell' trouble. Trouble is met with the gun in hand. The civilian has a different problem. He will usually be met by an attacker with a weapon already drawn. The felon is not always armed on a daily basis, but arms himself when actually on the move to commit a crime. He will attack with the gun in hand or concealed by only a newspaper or perhaps a hat. You must spot his advance and attack and not allow him to close distance. Distance favors the skilled practitioner of the combative arts. When practicing the draw, above all safety is the first consideration. The gun should not be loaded when practicing the draw in the home. A triple checked unloaded handgun will be used, and all who are in the home should be shown and convinced the handgun is not loaded. Even then, the gun should only be drawn against a backstop. You need not pull the trigger during these exercises. If the holster incorporates a safety snap the snap must be closed when the draw is begun, and the snap broken loose as part of the draw. I have seen many peace officers begin the draw, on the range, with an unsnapped safety strap, then work with the snap shut. This is wrong, and can be a killer.

The most efficient draw uses the least motion. A smooth draw is all important. Most of us will carry concealed, but the draw

Beginning the draw demands that the grip be finalized and the pistol is brought from the holster. (Kimber .38 Super, Milt Sparks holster.)

The pistol has cleared the leather and is going forward to meet the support hand

The two hands come together just in front of the belt and the gun is pulled forward

should be accomplished without the covering garments during the first few attempts. Get the basic movement down before advancing to the more difficult task of drawing from concealment. The draw begins with the hands relaxed in front of the body. The elbow of the strong side arm is shot to the rear, while the firing hand scoops the gun from the holster. The hand comes from underneath the holster, grasps the handgun butt and confirms the grip, and lifts the gun from the holster. To move to the gun from above, confirm the grip, and then draw is measurably slower. Be certain the grip is solid when the gun is drawn, the grip cannot be adjusted after the gun is draw or fumbling will result. The elbow meets the end of its travel-perigee is a good term-and the gun is now lifted from the holster. The firing hand meets the support hand just in front of the navel and the two hands are thrust forward. The gun is brought to the proper firing attitude and the sight picture is taken. A skilled shooter will be able to fire accurately about as soon as the gun breaks the plane between the target and the eyes.

Later, we will move to drawing from under covering garments. The hand approaches the line of the body and slides under the covering garment when a jacket or coat is worn. Care is taken not to snag the garments as the gun is drawn. In the case

The pistol is on target and ready to fire

of an inside the trousers holster, the shirt must be lifted up. Often, the weak side hand can be used to perform this task. As you will see, anytime we leave behind a standard strong side carry there are problems to be addressed. It is necessary for concealed carry, but whenever possible the strong side holster should be selected.

The crossdraw draw is different and requires more training. Crossdraw holsters are discussed later in the book. They have a place and are favorites of a number

In the above illustration, we begin a crossdraw from a DeSantis SkyMarshal holster

of experienced individuals. They are not for everyone. The disadvantages and advantages are discussed in the holster section. When drawing from a crossdraw holster, the hand reaches across the body and takes a proper firing grip. The gun is lifted from the holster and twisted under the support arm. Ideally the weak arm should be held out of the way of the strong side arm. The weak arm then moves forward to support the firing hand. The shoulder holster draw is much the same, except

This shooter is executing a solid, well defined Weaver stance

the support arm is held up and away at a much higher angle for safety. Neither is as fast as a strong side carry from an upright position. When seated the crossdraw has an advantage.

The ankle holster is often utilized by peace officers to carry a backup or second gun. This is a time honored practice and a true lifesaver. The ankle holster is so slow, however, it has been called the Dead Man's Draw. From a standing start, this is a difficult draw. However, when seated in a vehicle or when you are down on the ground, the ankle holster is a very fast draw. It should not be the primary carry, but is a very good secondary weapon location. I carried my backup handgun in an ankle holster for most of my police career, beginning with a Smith and Wesson .38, then moving to a Charter Arms .44 Special and finally a Kahr .40 caliber pistol. I practiced the draw many times.

To draw from the ankle holster while standing, I found the best course is to kneel on the strong side knee, simultaneously pulling the trousers leg up on the weak or holster side. The gun is then drawn. An alternate draw is usable if a wall is nearby. Simply lean against the wall and quickly bring the gun to the hand by raising the leg, carefully pulling the trousers leg up. When seated, the ankle holster is easily accessed by the firing hand. I have seen quite a few officers seated in the vehicle, interviewing subjects who stood outside the car, with their hand on the gun. When seated, the ankle holster is also very handy. Pocket carry is far from my favored carry. Just the same, I have executed quite a few draws from a pocket holster in order to qualify the best technique. The process is simple-slip the hand in the pocket, angle the holster to trap it so the gun and holster to not come out together, and then draw the gun. However, we do not get a good grip on the gun. If you place your hand in your pocket and make a fist, you will be unable to draw the weapon. The gun must be accessed smoothly with an open hand.

STANCE
The Weaver remains the best off hand position in my opinion.

However, the isosceles, which is basically thrusting the gun in front of you, is also a good choice for many shooters. I like the Weaver in that the shooter is bladed to the target and the Weaver seems more friendly to those of us who use body armor. However, when moving in the home or when moving in a search down a

The Weaver stance gives a good, tight control of any handgun. The 9mm, such as the Accurate Plating and Weaponry High Power, can be held practically motionless

wall, the Weaver is more complicated and sometimes conflicts with movement. I have seen a move away from the Weaver, but it is just as good a stance today as when Colonel Cooper first promoted the stance, some forty years ago.

FIRING POSITIONS

The off hand firing position is the most common, but there are others that offer real utility. When caught in the open, away from cover, locking into a kneeling position can be an aid to accuracy. I drop to the firing side knee and draw my weak side knee up. The weak side or support elbow locks on the weak side knee, giving a stable firing platform. Some students will find kneeling hopeless, for many reasons, but the student that can use kneeling well will find accuracy greatly improved. Kneeling fire is especially a good choice when firing around or just over cover. I have devoted quite a bit of time to learning the kneeling shot. At one time, certain qualification exercises demanded kneeling position firing. I fired at twenty five yards, but went to prone at fifty yards. For the student with a definite

This is the kneeling firing position. Using this solid position, you can hit well past fifty yards with practice

danger of confronting felons at long range-and this would include any peace officer and especially school guards——kneeling positions should be practiced.

Prone firing positions are slower to assume and much slower to break out of and become mobile again, but offer extremely stable firing platforms. When caught in the open, or when firing from certain types of cover, prone is ideal. To assume prone firing position, draw the handgun and present it well in front of your body. Move forward and support your body with the weak side hand. The hand is held forward and both hands meet. The gun is supported by the weak hand arm. The legs can be splayed aimlessly or one crossed over the other, which seems to work well. What is most important is that the head is rested against the biceps of the strong side shooting arm. If the head is held erect, blood flow to the brain is interrupted. Vision blurs, the neck cramps, and discomfort becomes a real problem. With the head resting upon the arm, a prone firing position can be held for some time comfortably. The prone position is sometimes overlooked, but can be used beneficially against threats at long range. Extraordinary shooting can be done at fifty yards or even more with an accurate handgun.

SITTING BRACED

This is a position promoted by the late Elmer Keith, a well known handgun experimenter and superb long range pistol shot. The back is placed against a wall, tree, or other solid object. The knees are drawn up in front of the body and the handgun is placed forward of the knees with the arm bones resting on the knees. With care and deliberation this is a very solid hold. Good shooting can be done with little discomfort or fatigue. I am not certain this position has any utility in self defense, as the body is exposed in a vulnerable position to any we are firing at. It is worth exploring as it can be a very accurate position. Recently, at the Spartanburg City Police Club range, I was able to fire a five round group which measured a mere two inches at a long fifty yards. I used the sitting braced position, a Czech CZ 75 pistol, and Black

Hills 115 grain ammunition. This is an outstanding performance from the shooter, handgun, and ammunition. I find the setting position comfortable and solid, but its tactical application limited.

COVER

One of the first rules in taking cover is to learn that you cannot draw and move. You can draw, then move to cover, or move to cover and draw, but the draw conflicts with movement. A dash to cover and a following draw is usually the best option, but keep your mind open.

I have often said that if you do not get to cover or take your man down in the first three seconds your battle is over. Cover is important. Those who take cover survive with few exceptions. It is important to know the difference between cover and concealment. Cover is anything that can be put between your body and a bullet.

This is an ideal position for accurate fire. This large tree will stop even high powered rifle fire

You must know the capabilities of both the bullet and common cover. A vehicle engine block will stop even an elephant rifle. A car door will stop most handgun calibers but few rifle calibers. You must develop a good understanding of the difference between cover and concealment. A sheet on a clothesline or brush may be good concealment, but they

This shooter has wisely chosen a large tree for cover

offer nothing in the way of cover. Cover is something that stops the bullet. There are numerous tricks concerning cover that peace officers learn. One is don't walk in the middle of a road or alley, even a dirt road on a search. Stay to one side and your outline is much harder to pick out or to take a bead on. This makes a great deal of difference when someone is attempting to find an aiming point. When moving into rooms, do not stand dead in the center of the doorway. Try to break around corners, or 'slice the pie' as we call it. This is simply looking at one area of the room or area at a time, being certain it is clear, and then moving on. I cannot over stress the importance of cover.

As an exercise, it is profitable to take a hard look at the various forms of cover you might fine in the various businesses and walkways you frequent on a daily basis. You may be surprised how much cover is out there in the world.

NIGHT SHOOTING

The majority of police shootings take place in dim light, but not total darkness. Civilian shootings are often more of the same. With street lights and vehicles lights so much a part of the nocturnal scene, true darkness is seldom found. Just the same, night combat is a serious tactical problem that must be addressed. There are numerous techniques and tactics that work, but they center upon two goals, identification and illumination. It is imperative we identify our target before firing. We cannot simply let rounds fly in the dark. I have actually read articles that recommended just that!

With titles such as 'alley cleaning' these brave souls described firing at gun flashes and other tactics best reserved for Israeli police actions in Lebanon.

Most night actions will take place at relatively short range. Body position and aiming will allow you to handle most of these battles. Familiarity with the handgun will bring you into the proper firing position and allow you to prevail at close range. When the range is a little longer the problem is more severe. A rough outline of the sights may serve at arm's reach but not just outside conversational distance. Two aids to night shooting exist which address different concerns. Target acquisition, identification and illumination is addressed by light, powerful flashlights. Hitting that target in the dark is addressed by self luminous iron sights. Proper illumination can offer a clear view of the gun's sights, but not always. An invaluable addition to any fighting handgun is the self luminous iron sight, commonly known as night sights. Night sights fea-

ture radioactive tritium sealed in a glass ampule. This ampule is topped
by a synthetic sapphire which concentrates the light of the miniature
nuclear furnace into a small but intensely bright dot. This is the source
of illumination for the night sight. These sights appear in air as green
'cat eyes'. Even in less than dark situations, such as the dim halls of
an apartment they work well. My personal .45 is fitted with a set
from Wilson Combat. The night sight picture is go good my night
work is on a par or even better than work in bright light, given an
adequate view of the target. The most common night sight configu-
ration is the three dot. In this type, the front sight is one part of the
dots and the rear sight has two dots. Alternatives exist. I have used
the bar dot type extensively. In this type, the front dot appears over a
horizontal bar set in the rear sight. An interesting and effective alternative is the Heinie 8 ball. This sight uses a large front dot over a
small rear, giving excellent results in every test I have undertaken.
The aforementioned sights are custom models. Many factory pistols,
especially the popular Glock, Beretta and SIG pistols are available
with high quality self luminous iron sights. These sights are a worthwhile addition to any handguns, some would say a necessity. If you
own an older model handgun, even a revolver, a shop that offers
quality retrofit of night sights is the Action Works.

The special drills developed for night shooting center upon
marrying a light but powerful light to the handgun. Modern handguns often incorporate rails into the lower frame that allow the
mounting of a powerful white light. Just the same, most of us
will find the stances which allow two hand fire while holding
the gun in one hand and the light in the other the most profitable.
I have included illustrations of the Harries technique, the most
common and widely accepted.

In the Harries the backs of the hand are touching. The handgun
is pointed normally. The light end of the flashlight extends from the
back of the hand. The thumb presses the momentary switch to turn
the light on. The tactic used is to tap the switch when you wish to
illuminate a target. Moving into this firing position becomes second
nature with appropriate practice. This means a minimum of five hundred successful moves into the Harries. The key components are

that the back of the hand is locked against the other and that the wrist are kept pressed together. This is by no means as rock solid as the Weaver and a normal two hand hold, but this type of grip can be used successfully in dim light.

To execute the Harries quickly, the gun hand is thrust forward and the weak hand, which has drawn the light, is thrust under the strong side arm quickly, sliding up into the proper position. The back of each hand is

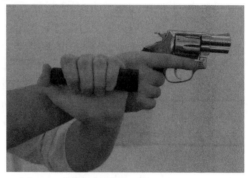

A close-up of a proper Harries stance

locked against the other. I have used the Harries operationally on numerous occasions, firing once. It works and works well. Once the hands are in position if they are allowed to slide or wobble the support can cause the firing hand to slide into the support hand, causing a malfunction. A tight grip is needed at all times.

There are alternate techniques which include thrusting the gun forward in one hand and the light in the other. They may prove suitable at very short range, but the Harries is by far the superior.

There are a number of lights which offer real utility in fighting at night. I have enjoyed excellent use with Streamlight products, especially the Scorpion. It is strong and effective. Diamond Products offers numerous lights and attachments for both long arms and handguns that offer robust performance at a reasonable price. The first rule of a gunfight is have a gun, but the second rule for night fighting is have a light.

MALFUNCTION CLEARANCE DRILLS

Despite the best care and lubrication of a handgun, there are times when the firearm may malfunction. Some malfunctions are related to the firearm itself, but most will be ammunition or operator related. There are several simple drills which will address most of the problems encountered. Some malfunctions are more complicated than others. True jams are rare, but misfeeds are not. The following drill is designed to address a failure to fire due to a bad round, commonly called a DUD, or a feedway malfunction.

The drill is executed as follows:

TAP   The bottom of the magazine is tapped aggressively, making certain the magazine is fully seated.

RACK   The slide is racked to the rear, clearing a malfunctioning cartridge. Interesting, my son has noted the US Military now teaches that the gun be tilted sideways during this drill, allowing the dud or malfunctioning round to fall free.

BANG   We fire.

An alternate drill is the Nichols drill. Taught first by trainer Larry Nichols, this drill also replaces the magazine.

The procedure is as follows:

The slide is locked to the rear

The magazine is ripped from the gun and discarded
and

A new magazine is inserted, the rear of the slide is grasped, and the slide released. The gun is then ready to fire. This drill

addresses more problems than the TAP RACK BANG drill but is

predicated upon the availability of a spare magazine. Another good reason to carry at least one spare gunload. TAP RACK BANG will solve practically any problem, but the Nichols drill is a respectable alternative.

Contrary to popular belief, revolvers can malfunction and fail to fire. When the revolver fails to fire, the first thing to do is to slap the cylinder shut and be certain it is in fact locked in the frame. If the gun has fired once or twice and stops firing, a high primer or an over pressure round could have stopped the action. Sometimes, a bullet can jump forward out of the case in recoil and tie the gun up. There are limited options. The only thing to do is to slap the cylinder shut if it is not completely closed, or in the case of a high primer or excess pressure lockup, hold the cylinder latch open and smartly rap the cylinder open. Even if you get the gun open, a true over pressure round may be difficult to extract. These things happen and should be planned for. I am unaware of a revolver malfunction during gunfight, but have seen a number on the range. I hope it remains that way.

CHAPTER NINE
ADVANCED TACTICS

Moving past basic range work we find advanced tactics. It is easy to overtax the shooter and his or her skill level by introducing multiple targets and unrealistic speed into range practice. By the same token, there are fast moving episodes in personal defense that have to be addressed. Gritty, short range struggles for

the handgun are also a possibility. We must have at least some idea of the problem and how to best answer each tactical necessity. Once you are in the fight it is too late to learn.

The retention position

This is an illustration of the retention position is very important to the armed combatant. This position allows the shooter to keep the pistol away from the hands of the adversary at close range, yet instantly ready. The elbow is locked in to the rib cage and the pistol held securely, finger off the trigger. The handgun can be fired from this position providing the shooter has sufficient grip and the slide can clear our clothing. In searches or when covering a hostile individual the retention position has much merit, but must be practiced to be effective. It is designed to enhance retention of the handgun.

THE APPLEGATE DRILL
The Applegate drill is a formidable short range drill designed to provide combat ability with a minimum of training. It accomplishes that well. The course of action is simple.

The handgun is drawn and smoothly moved on target. The instant the front sight breaks the plane between the shooter's eyes and the target, the pistol is fired. This is not point shooting or instinctive shooting, the sights are used. This is a tremendous tactic at short range, one which gives real speed when needed. I advocate two hand aimed fire when possible but at three to seven yards the Applegate can be very effective. Before you scoff at this drill, practice with a few times and compare it to anything else you may use at short range. Firing below eye level does not work except at contact range and two hand holds take a few seconds to assume. The Applegate drill should be in every serious shooter's tactical arsenal.

HOSTAGE RESCUE

Hostage rescue drills are routinely practiced and sometimes executed by SWAT teams. Often, they have access to precision rifles. Sometimes, the pistol is the weapon of choice. Home invasion robberies and kidnap attempts are common enough that the hostage rescue drill should be practiced. Of all drills that may be attempted, this is the one with the most peril if it is not accomplished correctly when the time comes to use it for real. If you have not mastered the basics and are not certain of your skills never attempt this type of shot. You cannot rely   upon skills you cannot demonstrate. The drill means just what it says hostage rescue. You are shooting the hostage taker who may be in close proximity to a family member or your partner. The only course of action is an immediate action drill. The bridge of the nose is the aiming point. Lower, and the jaw may absorb the impact of the bullet, higher, and the bullet may simply bounce around under the scalp. Yes, such things happen. It was not a rescue shot, but I am aware of a shooting- and I personally examined the aftermath- in which an adversary   took a 110 gr. .38 Special on the forehead. He was knocked out but recovered - the bullet flattened out on the skull! Modern bullets are better we hope but the cranial shot is by   no means always a sure thing. This is the shot that takes the greatest amount of nerve and can be the most important. Practice until you can pull the shot off on demand at five to ten yards, and be certain of the point of impact or your load versus the point of impact indicated by the sights.

As an example, we have discovered the .223 rifle strikes about six inches low at seven yards, making hostage rescue at this range dubious at best. Be certain of your weapon and ammunition. This is something skilled operators dread to undertake but the basics should be understood.

FIRING AT CROWDED TARGETS

Sometimes, you may have to fire at an adversary who is among several people. This is a nerve racking shot, and much practice should be undertaken. Range shots tend to be too easy in my opinion. When have we met an adversary in a wide field, alone? This is the type of shot that demands precision and finesse. You may wish to practice dropping to kneeling and firing upward so that the bullet does not exit the intended target and strike someone behind him. When you consider such problems, think tactical!

MOVING TARGETS

Moving targets are not as difficult as they appear. First of all, the ranges in handgun fights are short. Bullets are fast. But poor shooting makes for misses. The most important thing to remember is to swing with the target and carefully squeeze the trigger, holding the sights on the leading edge of the target. When you press the trigger, continue to move do not stop the gun short. This will jolt the gun and you will miss. Carefully moving with the target will produce hits at moderate range, given concentration. Remember, roll with the target and control the trigger. The further off the center the target is, the less you are squared to the target, the greater the problem. Moving targets really separate the skilled shooter from the novice. With practice, hitting moving targets is not so difficult. Shooting while on the move is another matter.

When you are forced to move in action, remember that some movements conflict. Drawing the gun conflicts with motion and you may be better served by dashing for cover, then drawing the gun. Just the same, I have enjoyed moderate success in moving and shooting on the range. It is dangerous to practice, in a sense, and probably not worthwhile. Still, by moving to cover and keeping the hand and arm in line you can possibly fire and strike the target if a lot of practice in trigger compression and sight picture is behind it. This is really what matters. If you have not mastered the basics of trigger compression and sight picture and sight alignment, these advanced tactics are worthless.

ANTI TERROR DRILLS

We have already discussed one anti-terror drill. The hostage rescue shot is among the most commonly practiced of all drills. So is shooting while moving. There are others. As an example, I enjoyed a lively debate with a man of great experience considering the famous Secret Service Drill. When a principal is attacked, the Secret Service covers the protected individual's body with their own. He has his own ideas but I bow to conventional wisdom. However, a tactic that has worked well for the SAS is startlingly effective. Our allies in England have used this operationally, notably in Malta. So have the Israelis. The tactic is to run at the terrorist at first sight, firing as you go. Few if any terrorists have the stomach for a fair fight. When a terrorist is surrounded by victims, this tactic diverts all of his attention to the person shooting at him. The goal is to force him to defend himself rather than shooting hostages while the operator who is moving toward him, firing, takes him out. The SAS, armed with Browning High Power pistols with ball ammunition, have done very good work with this tactic.

We have to remember the words of

Running at a terrorist!

Benjamin Netanyahu, one of the greatest experts on terror to ever live. His brother, Jonathan, was an Israeli Commando leader and the sole military casualty of the Entabbe raid. Netanyahu remarked that the single hardest part of an anti terror operation is not to let go with everything you have but to fire accurately. This drill is presented simply to show what a well trained individual is capable of. The person demonstrating the technique is a professional solider. He has been awarded numerous commendations including the General's Medal and been named Soldier of the Cycle. While most men lose weight in basic training, he added twenty pounds of rock solid muscle. His comments on this drill, "It is possibly one of the best suited to the task of drawing attention away from hostages and petrifying the enemy."

When moving, the gun is fired as the strong side foot hits the ground. At moderate ranges, from five to seven yards, accuracy was excellent. Even at longer ranges accuracy certainly was good enough to show a trained operator could develop this tactic to a high degree of accuracy. It is obvious that a sedentary person or anyone out of shape could never execute these drills effectively. To the men and women of our armed forces, a thousand yard sprint with a fifty pound pack is no challenge, nor is a six mile hike or a three mile run. Once you reach that standard you may attempt to equal their feats. But my mother and your elderly father will not be able to attempt such tactics. Keep the situation in perspective and strive for a personal best. That is all we can hope for, and the majority of the time it is enough.

CHAPTER TEN
HOLSTER SELECTION

For all around utility, we probably need two guns, a big gun and a small gun. But for those guns we need a minimum of two holsters each. A holster for concealed carry can be an inside the waistband or high ride belt holster, suitable for use in warmer climates. For wear under a light jacket, a strong side belt holster is desirable. Discretion requires weapon concealment. There are levels of concealment that should be understood.

A plainclothesman is not as concerned with concealment as an officer working true deep cover, and a citizen should go to greater lengths to conceal his weapon. In areas with a true four season climate, concealment becomes seasonal. If you live in Miami, Florida the weather is pretty constant and the same would apply in Anchorage, Alaska. For most of us different rules apply at different times of the year. I have tested numerous holsters over the years, many of obvious refinement, and many have an outstanding lineage. Whenever possible the strong side belt holster is the best choice. There should be a good reason for leaving the belt holster behind. The Kramer belt scabbard is among the better choices. The Blocker ST 17 is a good choice that also allows crossdraw carry, making it a versatile holster. Michael Taurisano has

This Medallion .45 from Armscorp is sheathed in a Vega holster, among the best of Italian leather. This is world class and first class at once

perfected his belt holster, and this is among my favorites. The High Noon Topless is another good option. For heavy handguns, the Alessi DOJ gives excellent support and is comfortable for long periods of wear. Ken Null's shell horsehide Speed

Scabbards are good for under the coat carry but his Gibraltar offers better concealment, riding closer to the body. It is all a matter of needs and body type, as well as personal style. When we can use a scabbard type holster, they offer the apex of speed and security. The proven pancake style hugs the body more closely, giving better concealment.

A popular option with professional, especially martial artists, is the crossdraw holster. The crossdraw is worn on the weak side and the strong hand reaches across the body to access the weapon.   If this seems slower than the shooting the elbow to the rear draw used with the strong side holster, you are correct.   There is also some concern the butt of the handgun is at least as accessible to an assailant as to the user.   That is why men of experience normally carry the crossdraw. As an example, if you are aware of the holster's faults, you can practice dropping the weak side elbow to protect the pistol from a gun grab, and have the strong hand free for blows. The advantage of the crossdraw is that the holster is accessible when seated.

If you spend your time in a vehicle or behind a desk the crossdraw is a good choice. The butt of the gun does not print on outer clothing when you stoop or bend. A properly designed crossdraw offers excellent concealment.

If you are seated and feel threatened, your gun hand can be practically on the weapon at all times. The strong side holster is more difficult to access when seated. A disadvantage of the crossdraw is that the draw is across the body of the adversary, not into it. In other words when you are squared to an adversary, and draw from the strong side position, the gun swings across the body. You have to stop the swing in the middle of the target. When drawing from the strong side position you cover the adversary from feet to head, affording more probability of a hit if the shot is less than perfect.

The crossdraw should never be discounted. Carefully consider your needs before considering any design, but for many of us the crossdraw has given good service for many years.

The shoulder holster is often seen as a racy, sexy holster.

These are not the right reasons for adopting this holster. The shoulder holster requires an extensive acclimation period. Some users never adapt to the shoulder holster. The constriction felt in wearing the holster simply is uncomfortable for many of us. Only the best examples should be chosen. The shoulder holster is difficult to adjust, and the straps can print on the outer clothing. That being said there are a number of good designs. The DeSantis New York Undercover and the 024 are good choices. Either generally offers good fit or adjustment, and a relatively quick draw. The advantages of this type are that the weight of the gun is kept off the hips and back. If you have a lower back or hip problem the shoulder holster can be a good choice with many of the inherent advantages of the crossdraw.

Among the most practical of all concealment holsters is the inside the trousers or inside the waistband holster. (IWB) The IWB rides between the body and the belt, offering good concealment. A relatively long heavy firearm can be concealed readily in this manner.

Even a short covering garment is sufficient to conceal the butt of a handgun carried in the IWB holster. Some report discomfort in wearing this holster and it does ride rather close to the body, hard against the muscle. Some experimentation is in order to find the best place to carry the IWB, but most of us end up carrying the pistol just behind the right hip. The long flat autopistol works best with this carry. When using an IWB holster, be certain to choose a quality rig that will protect both the gun and the shooter. A soft fabric or suede design will never work. These holsters collapse after the gun is draw. The pistol cannot be reholstered without loosening the belt and pants, something to be avoided when we are handcuffing a suspect or when a false alarm is over and we wish to reholster the handgun. Many IWB holsters have a plastic clip that slips over the belt. I cannot recall the times someone has told me they drew the weapon and a cheap holster of this type came away with the weapon. A well designed IWB should have a strong welt at the mouth for holstering and retention. This welt also prevents the weapon from rubbing against the body, a major source of irritation for many users.   The holster should be of good leather in order to wear long and comfortably.   A horsehide IWB is never a bad option.   The original top flight IWB came from Milt Spark's leather and it was a Bruce Nelson design.   Although both men are no longer with us the shop still turns out the original design. The Summer Special features a reinforced holster mouth, double or single loop belt attachment depending upon the exact model, and a strong spine as well as a sight track for ease of draw. Frankly, these holsters leave nothing to be desired.

I have seen a move in recent years to more rigid leather, especially from high end shops such as Alessi.   Lou Alessi uses a tunnel loop rather than a belt loop, which is a great aid in stability.   Sure it takes a little more time to mount but if you a are a professional wearing a holster and gun combination for ten to twelve hours a day, the Alessi is a good choice.   There are a number of modern designs that incorporate a strong spring steel belt clip and seem to work well. One of these is the Saigon Belt Clip from Graham Gunleather.   This minimalist design is a cut away that weighs scant ounces, but has given acceptable results in holstering my Commander .45. For those who are situationally armed, not armed on a 24-hour basis, this is an acceptable option. When choosing a holster, the watchword is quality. A well made holster of good material means everything. This is the

Note excellent fit and finish of Wild Bill's holster and belt combination, top, followed by Kramer and Don Hume belts

difference between a trusted friend and a chafing nuisance.

The belt

It is a waste to purchase a quality holster unless a purpose designed belt is used with the holster. A sturdy gun belt will keep the holster in place. The holster must be locked solidly to the belt. When holstering the gun, the holster must remain in the same place during movement. When marrying the holster and the belt always thread the belt properly through the holster loops, never skipping a belt loop in the trousers. This will make for a stable platform in drawing and a much more comfortable platform during daily movement. The less movement, the better.

CHAPTER ELEVEN
SHOOTING VEHICLES &
SHOOTING FROM VEHICLES

Vehicles are a necessity of life. If you question the inclusion of this chapter, consider this— two of the most powerful handgun calibers available in semi autos, the .38 Super and the .357 SIG, were designed expressly to address the problems of felons behind vehicle cover. Half of the FBI's shootings have involved felons behind cover, much of it vehicular in nature. Drive-bys, car-jackings and other assaults may require that you fire into a vehicle. You may even be forced to fire from inside your own vehicle. The problems are many. Vehicles are far from bullet proof but they are resistant to bullet impact. We must carefully consider shot placement and address the problem with fore-thought.

Shooting vehicles
If you fire into a vehicle the bullet can go anywhere. Anyone in the vehicle can be struck, so firing into a vehicle should only be done in the direst circumstances. Still, it happens often. At one time, eleven of thirteen shootings I researched in a single year involved felons in vehicles.

The common small pistol calibers are hopeless against windshield glass and car doors. Only beginning with the .38 Special and 9mm Luger do we have a fighting chance. According to a special test program I conducted for Police Magazine, the single best cartridge and load combination for overall effectiveness against a vehicle is the Hornady 124 grain XTP in .357 SIG caliber. This load offered good penetration and the XTP proved to expand in tissue simulant even after impacting windshields. The Gold Dot loads also did well. My personal favorite, the .45 ACP, certainly was not a bad performer, but was acceptable given good delivery.

As far as modern vehicles are concerned, small and large

examples are much the same. Most have interior door bracing and window regulators. The regulator is the mechanism that moves the window up and down. Even the most energetic handgun bullet will stop dead on a regulator, given a center hit. It is profitable to fire near the top of the door where there is less bracing when engaging a felon behind a vehicle door. The dead center of four door car doors is usually the strongest braced section, and just forward of center on two door vehicles. A high velocity 9mm caliber bullet can do reasonably well against this type of cover, but multiple shots will be the rule.   A m o n g the most impenetrable of all obstacles are the rear doors of full size station wagon and SUV type vehicles. These constructs will soak up most handgun bullets. There is little profit in attempting to place a bullet through them. On the other hand most passenger cars are vulnerable from the rear. Providing the bullet does not strike the spare tire or jack, a bullet will normally cut through the trunk readily.

Vehicle glass is hard on a bullet. The door glass and rear glass will normally shatter when hit by a bullet, but the windshield is another matter. The windshield can tear a hollowpoint bullet apart or deflect a non-expanding bullet. Several loads I have tested, and this includes the .45 ACP, separated on the windshield, the jacket sticking in the glass and the core lying in the front seat. These loads are fine for defense use against individuals who are not clad in leather jackets at any rate, but not suitable for use by peace officers who make encounter felons behind cover. The Winchester SXT, Hornady XTP, Remington Golden Saber, Federal Hydra Shock, Speer Gold Dot and the Black Hills line are well suited for use against vehicles, as well suited as any handgun ammunition for use against vehicle bodies. Full metal jacketed ammunition offers no real advantage. 9mm and .45 hard ball have a profile that glances off braces and is not well suited to penetration of sheet metal. An exception may be the .40 caliber Smith and Wesson flat point full metal jacketed bullet. I have experienced extraordinary penetration with this bullet, using Black Hills factory loads. It may behoove one to carry a spare magazine of these loads just in case. The rule is to shoot straight and aim for what may be a more vulnerable area. But best of all, take cover that will stop the bullet the adversary is launching at you.

If forced to fire from your own vehicle, you have another set of problems. If you fire from inside your vehicle and the bullet does not exit it may bounce back and wound the shooter. A Sheriff's Deputy in my jurisdiction attempted to fire from his vehicle and the bullet struck his dash, bouncing back and wounding this individual. If you are in your vehicle and able to leave the best course of action is to leave the area of the problem immediately.

If you must fire from a vehicle, be certain the gun muzzle clears the body of the vehicle

When firing at the adversary from outside the vehicle, we should understand that the bullet fired from a handgun would travel at a downward angle when fired at an adversary. The short ranges involved seldom call for any major deflection, however. On the other hand, when you are firing from inside the vehicle through the windshield the problems are much more pronounced. I have performed extensive test firing from inside vehicles at targets at various ranges, and when firing through vehicle glass the problem is that bullets strike high in relation to the point of aim. At twelve feet distance if you aim for the midsection the bullet will strike in the upper chest. A firearm that will pull five shots into one hole at fifteen feet will suffer five to six inches dispersion in a carefully fired group fired through glass. Not only that, the problem of firing glass chards in your eyes is very real. This is not theoretical. One of the most dramatic photos I have seen from Wounded Knee SD is of a FBI a agent vehicle with five evenly spaced .38 caliber bullets holes, fired from inside the vehicle at American Indian Movement operators firing from a moving vehicle. A vehicle is good cover from handgun bullets but the best choice is to use the vehicle to escape.

CHAPTER TWELVE
CARRYING SPARE AMMUNITION

Carriers from Wilson Combat, BCO, and Glock. All can do the job

Most handgun fights take place in a few seconds and few rounds are fired. If you do not get to cover or take your adversary out in the first three seconds your fight is over I have often said. Just the same, there have been times when more than the gun load of ammunition is needed. And, once the hostility is over, we wish to reload. We should carry spare ammunition. While some feel more comfortable with two gun loads I think one should be sufficient for any fight short of an invasion of another country. The proven method of carrying a spare magazine is to wear it in a leather holster just behind the weak side hip. The spare magazine carrier should be compact and sturdy, presenting the magazine for a rapid draw. Double magazine carriers for the slim Colt 1911 magazine are not very obtrusive and may be a good option.

Carrying a revolver speed-loader is another problem the speed-loader is as bulky as a revolver cylinder and difficult to hang on the belt. AE Nelson makes a speed-loader carrier I have had good results with. It completely encloses the carrier, but the carrier can be quickly snapped open and the speed-loader grasped. Cunningham Custom Leather crafts one of the all time great speed-loader carries. This holder enfolds the speedload and simply rolls the loader into the hands when the snap is opened. The many shooters still using the revolver will appreciate this holder very much. In short while spare ammunition is not always needed it is never a bad idea. As an example, if we suffer a malfunction in the semi auto the magazine should sometimes be dumped to clear the gun, and we should have another magazine handy, just in case.

Don't neglect the spare gun load. It could be a life saver.

CHAPTER THIRTEEN
HANDGUN FINISHES

The choice in handgun finishes has never been more broad than today. You can even own a pink gun if you so desire.

The finish applied to any handgun is to protect the natural metal from rust, in the first consideration.

The secondary consideration is to protect the weapon from wear in normal use. If we practice as we should the pistol will see considerable wear from presentation from the holster. A tightly fitted holster can produce surface wear on a blued finish fairly quickly.

For most of the history of the handgun, simple rust blue has been the normal finish. A form of controlled rust, bluing can be attractive and reasonably long wearing. Nickeling was an early low maintenance finish fairly popu-lar over one hun-dred years ago. In my own situation, I have presented the handgun from cover as many as 3,000 times in one year. As a peace officer, I often practiced the draw

Bear Coat finish can be regarded as space age. This Pistol has seen much use but remains new

a dozen times or more a day. It doesn't take long.

Once, while on assignment in a rural area, I was assigned to watch a downed and live power line for over five hours. With no AM or FM radio, no reading material and little else to do, I drew and holstered the gun a hundred times or more! As may be ex-pected, I was a very fast young man after a few months of this type of action.

One of the only duty holsters that would stand up to this type of practice was the Don Hume, and I eventually wore one of these out!

When looking at a finish and the attributes it must possess, take a hard look at what the handgun must face. The elements, weather and holster wear are considerations. But the natural body chemicals are corrosive as well. I have turned several blue handguns brown in short order carrying them next to my body in deeper concealment. So, while a home defense weapon that will be carefully maintained might be acceptable with a blue finish, a weapon carried close to the body in a humid climate needs a more durable finish. We can choose the finish we wish to use in factory handguns, but we can also have an existing weapon replated or refinished, no matter what the original finish was.

Some shooters prefer a non reflective finish, which is fine but I think a moot point in a combat gun.   If you are shooting at someone I doubt the weapon's light signature under reflection will be a consideration.   Indeed, many old time cops fa-

This Taurus pistol is finished in NP 3 finish, which has rendered excellent results

vored nickel plated handguns, feeling that the gun's aggressive appearance was a key to compliance.

I strongly prefer a polished blue if blue is the finish selected. Matte blue finish is not as smooth and wears quite quickly. Some of the major makers have excellent finishes as issued. The SIG, Glock and Beretta pistols have excellent black finishes known by names such as SIGKOTE, Tenifer, and Bruniton. All work well. Nickel and chrome plate seem far less common these days. Hard chrome as applied by Accurate Plating and Weaponry is a good choice, hard and durable as well as attractive, but expensive. A P and W offers other finishes but this is my favorite. It is worth every penny!

As aluminum frames were a great step forward in the 1950s, stainless steel was a great advance in the 1970s. Stainless steel originally presented problems in galling but modern materials have solved these problems. Stainless steel is a good option, but stainless is just as its name implies— stain + less. Still, good quality stainless steel revolvers and autos are long lived given good maintenance.

A new breed of finishes combines Teflon technology and electroless nickel. Robar's NP 3 is among these. A finish I have had excellent results with is Rocky Mountain Arm's BearCoat. This finish is self-lubricating. If you attempt to lubricate the gun, oil will simply run off. I have enjoyed excellent results with a half dozen different handguns. Bear Coat is available in light and dark finishes and even camouflage. Bear coat is much more resistant to corrosion than chrome, while chrome resists wear better. This is a personal decision but in this day and age something other than simple blue is desirable. There is nothing wrong with the black tactical look. It is low key and non-reflective.

Wilson Combat offers a finish available Armor Tuff. This is another space age finish, offered on Wilson Combat's high end pistols. The obvious excellence of these handguns is an endorsement of the technology.

Overall, there is much to choose from in handgun finishes and several available to fit any need. I tend to favor low key, non reflective finishes such as Bear Coat for service handguns but there is nothing wrong with a high profile hard chrome finish on a personal gun you value highly.

CHAPTER FOURTEEN
FIGHTING AIDS

I do not like to applaud hardware with one voice and point out that it is the man or woman behind the gun with the other, but in fact there are a number of tools that give the qualified operator a real advantage in a fight. These tools should be carefully chosen. We have covered holsters, which are largely a matter of personal preference, as long as good choices are made. But there are a couple of items that can really be an aid to survival.

THE TACTICAL EAR

This little device amplifies sounds in the home or the street, allowing you to keep an ear open (!) during movement. Yet, if a gun fires, tiny baffles in the ear close, protecting your hearing. A number of tactical teams use this device, with excellent results. The

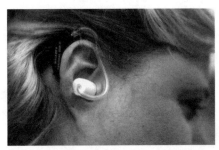

Walker's Tactical Ear is light-weight and durable, but really does the job

large muff type tactical ears are the best training aids I have yet discovered and cover both ears, while the small unit is carried in a single ear with an exception being the numerous operators who deploy one in each ear. When moving in the home or even in security work or police work, these 'ears' are great tactical aids. The ear muff types allow a trainer or instructor to carry on a conversation with his students without removing the muffs. Also called the Walker Game Ear, these devices are useful for hunting. None of us would be out of line keeping these muffs beside our bed at night. We can quickly don them and listen for an intruder, and if forced to fire we will not permanently damage our hearing. Overall, I like these 'Tactical Ears' both in concept and in implementation.

A second must have, and a solid adjacent to the handgun is a good folding knife. The folder can be an aid in retaining the weapon from a gun-grab. Properly wielded, the knife can prevent a gun grabber from grabbing your holstered handgun. If a felon grabs you and your gun from behind in the common arm across the neck tactic, a simple slash to the arm will move it quickly. I cannot overrate the importance of the back up knife as a tactical advantage. By the same token, on those occasions when we are forced to travel unarmed, the tactical knife is a good contact weapon. We should all have a continuum of force available, and have something between open hands and the firearm available. The knife can be a powerful blunt striker. Don't leave home without it.

KNIFE TYPES

There are numerous good folders. The Al Mar SERE is a favorite. For truly heavy duty use, the Buck Stryder is a first choice. When it comes to versatility, Spyderco is among the finest choice. But it seems that the choice of high speed low drag operators comes from Benchmade. You pay your money and you take your choice.

This is the author's Action Works 1911 and GT Knife - an excellent combination.

CHAPTER FIFTEEN
THE BEST FIGHTING HANDGUNS

While I believe that the person behind the gun is most important, there are a number of weapons types that unnecessarily limit shooters. Some modern weapons are a triumph of the technical over the tactical. There has never been more choice than today, and some of these choices are very bad, at least in my professional opinion. Some of the most capable handguns in the world have been in production for over ninety years. Others are barely a decade young. I will not recommend any weapon that I do not have extensive experience with. Bargain basement guns are not normally recommended. Just the same, a number of the weapons found in this chapter are surprisingly affordable. All I ask is 'When have you been sorry for buying quality?'

For the purposes of this review, I chose to break out old favorites and beg or borrow what I did not have on hand. It is obvious some weapons will not perform as well as the others, but some of these pistols are very light, or simply very handy. It is a fact that the Charter 2000 .44 Special Bulldog, a light revolver cannot run a combat course in the manner a Kimber .45 auto may, but I am glad to have each in my arsenal. I limited the test to fifty handguns. There could have been many more, but after reading this chapter you will have a good idea of the pluses and minuses of each weapon and weapon type. To validate my finding, I fired each weapon 100 rounds, a small number of rounds but one which gave us a good feel for the guns. In some cases, I have many thousands of rounds in the weapons. As for 1911 type handguns, a rough estimate shows I have well over fifty thousand rounds in this type, probably closer to sixty thousand in the last twenty years alone. These are my conclusions.

I do not use a machine rest. That would be a laughable test of a fighting handgun. Keeping in touch with reality, I fired the shots offhand at short range and from a solid weaver stance. This showed the sharp edges of the gun, muzzle flip, and any function problems properly. For the combat test, I fired a five shot group at ten yards as quickly as I could bring the front sight back into the rear groove after recoil and pull the trigger. I measured this group in inches. At some point, I also fired five rounds, seated, from a solid bench rest at 25 yards as the standard measure of a handgun's accuracy. Accuracy is not everything but does show proper care in manufacture. What follows are the facts concerning the best combat guns in the world.

Keep in mind the ten yard groups are combat groups, the twenty five yard groups, slow fire target groups.

REVOLVERS
#1 Smith and Wesson Model Ten Military and Police .38 Special
This revolver has the attributes of all revolvers. It is simple to manipulate and quite easy to use well. The grip shape fits most hands and the gun is light enough. This is as good a beginners gun as can be had, and a reasonable choice for any shooter. This is as powerful a cartridge and gun combination as the average shooter can handle.
Fired   100 rounds Winchester 158 grain SWC
10 yards   4.5 inches   25 yards   4.0

#2 Taurus 85 Stainless Steel
This is the quintesstial hideout. A five shot .38 Special revolver with a two inch barrel is light, easy to conceal, and quick into action. We found the action smoother than a similar Smith and Wesson and the sights broad and easily acquired in a speed drill. This is a good small revolver. Like all small .38s concentration and attention to detail are demanded for proper

A pair of excellent compact revolvers from Taurus; one a .38, the other, a .357

use, but the pistol can serve well in personal defense within it's range limitations.

Fired   100 rounds Black Hills 125 grain JHP

10 yards   6 inches   25 yards   5.5 inches

#3 Smith and Wesson Model 19, .357 Magnum, 2.5 inch barrel

This is a revolver that fits most hands well and has a smooth, easy to use action. The modern rubber grips soak up recoil well. As may be expected, with Magnum loads this is a gun with plenty of buck, kick, and muzzle blast. Still, first shot hit probability is excel-

The combat Magnum is light enough and smooth in action

lent. This is a revolver downed by many writers but appreciated by thousands of defense shooters across the world.

Fired   50 rounds .38 Special, Winchester 158 grain SWC

          50 rounds Black Hills .357 Magnum 125 grain JHP

10 yards (Magnums) 6.0 inches   25 yards   1.8 inches

#4 Ruger GP 100

Of all Magnum revolvers, this is possibly the most durable and the toughest. Most regard this weapon as too heavy for con-

stant carry. It would be a difficult gun to conceal. But for home or ranch use, or for defense against animals, this is a wonderful choice. The gun is handy and a bit slow into action, and rapid fire is simply a reasonable cadence. But

The rugged and accurate GP 100

the GP 100 is also very accurate, and a fine all around Magnum revolver. The Combat Magnum is faster into action and easier to handle, the Ruger, easier to control.

Fired   50 Winchester 145 grain Silvertip   50 Cor Bon 180
grain JSPs, the strongest known Magnum load.

10 yards	4.0 inches	25 yards	1.0 inch
		Cor Bon	.9 inch

#5 Smith and Wesson Combat Magnum

To my mind, this is the finest self defense revolver available. It is light enough for constant carry, has a good trigger action, and is very fast into action. The gun kicks more than some and may not be as rugged nor able to with-stand thousands of rounds of full power ammunition. But the revolver is accurate, fits small hands well, and does the business on demand. No one need apologize for deploying a revolver when it is the Combat Magnum.

Smith and Wesson Combat Magnum with a 4 inch barrel

Fired   100 rounds, Black Hills .357 Magnum 125 grain.

10 yards	3.5 inches	25 yards	1.5 inches

#6 Smith and Wesson L Frame

This revolver features a K frame grip frame and is over all beefed up, resembling the Ruger GP 100. I have yet to meet a shooter who swears by these revolvers as they did the Combat Magnum or the big frame Model 27 or Model 28. Still, few seem to curse them. I found the revolver's weight somewhat damp-ened recoil but predictably

The L Frame .357 Magnum from Smith and Wesson

it was not as fast into action as the K frame Model Nineteen or

Combat Magnum. Overall, the revolver is OK but I prefer the lighter Combat Magnum.

Fired   100 rounds Winchester Silvertip, 145 grain
Ten yards   5.5 inches   25 yards   2.0 inches

#7 Taurus Model 66

I purchased this revolver for a song at the pawn shop. I intended it to be a 'truck gun' but it shoots so well I have put it to all around use. It has taken game and guarded the homestead for years. It is the most accurate single revolver I have seen with the .38 Special Winchester FBI load, a load not noted for accuracy. Overall, this is a good handgun. I have not pushed it with heavy loads and it has performed beyond my expectations.

Fired   50 rounds Winchester .38 Special 158 SWC +P
        50 rounds Black Hills 125 grain .357 Magnum
10 yards (Magnums) 5.0 inches   25 yards   2.5 inches

#8 Taurus 82 .38 Special, three inch barrel

Beyond a shadow of a doubt this is one of the fastest handling, best balanced, and sure pointing revolvers ever made. Rapid fire control is compromised by light weight and thin grips but you should be on your man with the first shot with this revolver. It is a remarkable revolver in every way. Recoil is subdued even with +P loads, and the gun is

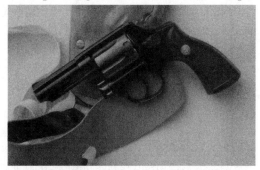

The Taurus 82 three inch barrel was impressive in balance and handling

fast on target. Slow fire accuracy is nothing to brag about, but this is a pure fighting handgun. For the revolver man, this is just about perfect. It is also available in .357 Magnum, even better. I found this gun for a song in the pawn shop but new versions are not very expensive.

Fired   50 rounds Federal 158 grain RNL

50 rounds Speer 125 grain Gold Dot

10 yards   5.0 inches   25 yards, Gold Dot   3.0 inches

#9 Smith and Wesson Model 36 Chief's Special

This is the primogenitor of the five shot .38 Special and still a very good choice. My revolver is smooth in action, with good sights and excellent balance. Like all small .38s control in rapid fire is difficult. Good trick shots can be made at long range with care and deliberation but that is not what combat hand gunning is about. This is a reliable, smooth revolver that demands much of the shooter.

Fired   100 rounds Federal 158 grain roundnose

10 yards   5.5 inches   25 yards   4.0 inches

#10 Charter 2000 Bulldog .44 Special

Here is a real pug of a gun. I have defended myself with an earlier version and the guns work better than range tests would tell us. For real self defense type shootings short range and very quick work-the Bulldog excels. The gun does kick and I admit the 100 rounds fired were a chore. Just the same, here is a gun with substantial power. Careful handloaders can raise the bar on power considerably.

Fired   Cor Bon 165 grain JHP +virtually the only suitable load
         for defense use in this gun, in this caliber.

10 yards   6.0 inches   25 yards   3.25 inches

#11 Charter Arms Off Duty

Here is a real candidate for the best concealed carry revolver of all. The hammer is fully enclosed by a geometrically designed grip frame. This humpback frame lowers the gun's bore axis and

aids in soaking up felt recoil. Even with heavy loads, this is a pleasant revolver to fire. It is light enough and the action smooth. The sights are good. There are no flies on this revolver. Modern CNC machinery really makes a difference between these guns and previous Charter efforts. This is a good revolver.

Fired   50 rounds, Speer Gold Dot 125 grain JHP +P
         50 rounds, Cor Bon 110 grain JHP +P
10 Yards (Gold Dot)   5.0 inches
25 yards (Cor Bon)   5.5 inches

AUTOMATICS
#12 Kel Tec .32

No, I don't like .32s, but if someone is going to carry this kind of gun it should be a good one. I am at 1,000 rounds on the Kel Tec with few malfunctions. The few I have experienced have been due to substandard or junk ammunition. With good ammunition this gun works well. It lacks true sights having only a small cut out on the slide, but it is easy to make hits on man sized targets to ten yards. And it will hit a man at 25 yards, but just where is the question. At intimate range, the gun has all of the accuracy needed. Perhaps the best backup or hideout, ounce for ounce, available.

Fired   100 rounds, Fiocchi ball
10 yards   6.5 inches   15 yards in deference to the gun's
                                 sights or lack of sights-

                                          8.0 inches

#13 Beretta .22 Long Rifle

I like this gun a lot. It is a ball to shoot and surprisingly accurate. If you cannot carry a full caliber gun for any reason or desire a small backup, this is a pistol that works and works well.

Maintain it with a high degree of cleanliness and lubrication and it will serve well. But rely on something larger.

Fired   100 rounds, Winchester Wildcat .22 RNL
10 yards   4.0 inches   2 5
yards   5.9 inches

#14 Kahr K 40

Kahr showed Europeans that Americans can make a world class pistol. And beat them at their own game. This is a wonderful pistol. The trigger is double action only but a very light, smooth version. The sights are good, the gun feeds anything, and is surprisingly pleasant to fire. It is a true purpose designed compact, not a cut down version of a service gun. This makes all of the difference in the world. I highly recommend this pistol. For those wishing to carry a light gun but not wishing to compromise power and reliability, the

The Kahr's performance is suprising, even in modern times

Kahr in .40 caliber is an unmatched choice. Mine rode as a backup for many years in an Alessi ankle holster, and as a primary weapon at other times. I can give no higher recommendation than that.

Fired   50 rounds, Black Hills 155 grain JHP
            50 rounds, Cor Bon 150 grain JHP

10 Yards (Black Hills)   5.0 inches
25 yards (CorBon)   2.2 inches

#15 EAA Witness

The Witness bears mention because it is relatively inexpensive but accurate and reliable. High capacity magazines are readily available at a fair price, and the pistol offers many good features. I appreciate the ability to choose either hammer down double action first shot or cocked and locked, safety on, first shot in the same pistol. The sights are a little too blocky but the pistol works, all we can ask for.

The Witness, top, is a clone of the CZ 75, bottom.

Fired   100 rounds Winchester USA, 124 grain

10 yards   3.4 inches   25 yards   4.0 inches

#16 CZ 75

The CZ 75 has an enviable, almost legendary reputation. The more I handle these pistols the more I am impressed. This is a reliable pistol, as might be expected of a favorite of the Soviet Spetsnazt. The pistol is so good it embarrasses some in the West, according to Colonel Jeff Cooper. He is right. While some of the copies and clones are OK the original CZ is quite a pistol. I highly recommend this weapon, with no reservations.

Fired   100 rounds Winchester USA 124 grain

10 Yards   2.9 inches   25 yards   '   2.25 inches

#17 Browning High Power

For many years I felt that the Colt 1911 was the fastest of all handguns to an accurate first shot. This remains true when the test is restricted to big bore handguns, but in a level test the Browning High Power has proven quicker, in my hands, to an accurate first shot than any other handgun. This remains true as long as the pistol is a modern version with the large pedal type safety. The pistol tested is highly modified. The pistol has been hard chromed, a speed safety added, and a trigger job performed. Trigger compression is a

The Browning Highpower, done up by Accurate Plating and Weaponry, is among the most accurate and reliable handguns.

smooth, light and lovely three pounds. The problem is of course this pistol is 'only' a 9mm. I have tremendous confidence in the .45 and not so much in the 9mm. But as far as reliability and combat ability can be measured, this custom 9mm is at the very top of the scale. The High Power can deploy with fourteen rounds, total, in the gun, it is small enough to conceal well, fits even small hands well, and handles +P ammunition well. There has been much good work done with the

High Power over the years, especially in the hands of the SAS in Britain, Ireland and Malta. If you are going to use a 9mm caliber handgun, use a good one. This is the best of the best.

Fired   50 rounds Winchester 124 grain ball, 50 rounds Winchester 127 gr. SXT +P+

10 yards   2.0 inches   25 yards   1.25 inches

#18 Glock M 22 .40 caliber

As we venture into the Glock pistols we have to burst your bubble, all Glocks are not alike. These pistols have significant differences in handling that many writers gloss over. The Glock trigger action is certainly usable as a combat arm. While classed as a double action only, reset is faster than many single action triggers and the compression is usually 5 to 5.5 pounds, quite usable. The blocky sights limit accuracy, but only past 15 yards. It is a simple matter to fit Novak, Heine or Wilson Combat high visibility sights. Or simply order your Glock with factory installed night sights. These sights have a much better sight picture and give the self luminous option. The Glock demands rigid uncompromising trigger discipline. The Glock has been likened to a single action pistol with no safety. This is true. There is no manual safety, only the trigger lever in the face of the trigger. The Glock does have a low bore axis and a well shaped grip frame, which makes it easy to shoot well. I have owned several Glocks in the past and went back to my 1911s and High Powers. Just the same, they are good combat guns providing the user is well aware of their demand for conscious, responsible gun handling.

The Glock Model 22 .40 is my personal choice among the Glock line. It is light enough, fires a good cartridge, and accurate enough for defense. I have fitted an array of sights to these guns, a Jarvis custom barrel, and even a Bar Sto barrel in .357 SIG. Overall, results have been good. I cannot recall a malfunction with any Glock 22.

Fired   50 rounds Winchester 155 gr. Target

50 rounds Winchester 155 gr. Silvertip

10 yards   3. 0 inches (Stip load)
25 yards (155 gr T)   3.4 inches

#19 Glock 23

This is the compact version of the Glock 22. Recoil is more no-
ticeable, but the trade-off in
compactness and easy
carriability is worthwhile. The
Model 23 is sometimes faster
into action and on target, depending upon the shooter. This
is a very good compact
weapon, with handling characteristics that are universally ap-
pealing.

The compact Model 23 is among the more popular
choices of armed professionals

Fired   100 rounds Winchester 165 grain SXT
10 Yards   3.5 inches   25 yards   4.0 inches

#20 Glock 30

Here is a gun I wanted to like very much but could not. I have
average size hands and short fingers, but many of the people who
examined this weapon had the same problem. This is the only Glock
I have ever fired in which I missed shots by not compressing the
trigger and the trigger bar set in the face of the trigger. This is a
compact version of the full size double column magazine Model 21
.45. It is simply too great a reach for most of us. Glock now has a
single column magazine .45, the model 36, that should be much better. It is one thing to control a gun under range conditions but another
to consider combat ability and retention on the street. The Model 30
is too big for most of us to use well.

Fired   50 rounds Winchester USA 230 gr. Ball
         50 round Black Hills 185 gr. JHP
Accuracy fired with Black Hills
10 Yards   5.0 inches   25 yards   4.0 inches

#21 Glock 26 9mm

I owned a Model 26 for some time. A ten shot 9mm no larger than a snubnose .38, this pistol has many good qualities. But keep the pistol in perspective. I have seen guards and Federal Agents carrying the Model 26 and the Model 27, the .40 caliber version, as holster guns or their primary weapons. Anytime you can carry the Model 23 or Model 22, you should. The Model 26 requires much

more effort to shoot well. The short grip and shorter than normal sight radius demand concentration. This is the snub .38 equivalent of the full size Glock and it will not shoot and handle as well as the full size pistols. With practice accuracy and control are excellent. The .40

This Glock has been custum tuned by Actions by T. Note the nickle slide

version is a bit harder to control but the preferred choice. The only malfunction I have ever experienced with a Glock came from a Model 26. There is a dip in the grip frame not found on larger Glock pistols. In recoil, with a +P load, my thumb locked the slide open, stopping a shooting string. Operator error? Sure, but I never experienced any type with the other Glocks. The Model 26 is a good hideout, but understand it's limitations. Choose a larger Glock when possible.

Fired   100 rounds, Black Hills 124 gr. JHP

10 Yards   4.3 inches   25 yards   2.9 inches

(With a solid rest, the Model 26 is accurate!)

#22 Glock 21 .45

All comments concerning the Glock 21 also apply to the Glock 20 in 10mm. The 10mm is sometimes more accurate and exhibits more muzzle flip with full power loads.

The Glock 21 has two sterling attributes, reliability and accuracy. Perhaps soft shooting should be applied as well. This is a .45 caliber pistol that kicks little, offering good control. The problem with this pistol is size. It is big, blocky, and difficult for the average hand to handle. Many shooters fire it well enough on the range, in controlled conditions, but have difficulty in controlling the pistol in rapid fire or in defending the weapon in retention drills. Still, large hands work well. Some women with small hands and long fingers can really get the most of this pistol. I did not experience the problem of properly pressing the trigger lever experienced with the Model 30, so there is a subtle difference in geometry in this weapon. The Model 21 holds 14 rounds of .45 ACP ammunition with law enforcement magazines, or 11 with modern magazines. This is a powerful reserve. The gun is hard to conceal but certainly light enough. Overall, a truly effective weapon for those with large hands. Just because that leaves me out doesn't mean I do not respect this pistol. It is a good one.

Fired   50 rounds Cor Bon 185 grain JHP

50 rounds Cor Bon 200 grain JHP

10 yards   3.9 inches   25 yards   1.8 inches

#23 Springfield XD 40

This pistol has very little in the way of a track record but as of this writing it is getting a lot of favorable ink and I thought I should include it in this review. The XD 40 is a polymer frame pistol that is similar to the Glock. However, the grip frame feels much more like the 1911. The pistol also features a grip safety. The pistol cannot be fired unless this grip safety is fully depressed. This is a good idea, and the device does not prevent rapid engagement of targets or fast handling. This does not take the place of a manual safety but it is fine as far as it goes. We found the XD 40 has acceptable sights, good reliability, and a decent trigger compression of about five pounds. In firing two examples for an extensive review at Gun Week, reliability was excellent. There were no malfunctions of any type no matter what the gun was fed. A clean bill of health? So far so good but I want to take a look at the gun in five years. I like the handling and system better than the Glock but the Glock is proven. That means much more at this time.

Fired   100 rounds Federal 155 grain Hydra Shock

10 Yards   4.0 inches   25 yards   3.5 inches

#24 Heckler and Koch USP

I have tested three of these pistols, all the compact versions and in 9mm, .40, and .45 calibers. The .45 is a bit large for my hands-again. I am going to hire a person with large hands to shoot for the

next book! But trust me, my hands are not that small and if I have problems with a gun so will most of you. However, the standard H and K offers hammer back cocked and locked carry, which means that I could shoot the big .45 very well. I simply ignored the double action option. The H and K is offered in

The H and K did very well, accuracy wise with all Black Hills loadings.

a confusing array or configurations, but I will make it simple. There are only three we need be concerned with. These are,

Double action only   A long pull for each shot

Double action, decocker   The pistol fires as a standard DA gun, and the safety is only a decocker.

Double action with a safety :

The final option is the one that makes the most sense to me. The pistol can be carried hammer down with the safety on. Many modern pistols have a slide mounted safety that is difficult to manipulate quickly. The H and K is frame mounted. This makes for much quicker and more sure handling. The pistol has the option of being carried hammer back, safety on, 1911 style. I like that. However, if you are a confirmed double action man consider this problem. When running a combat course with the decocker variant, the pistol must be decocked on the run. Even if you carry the gun hammer down, safety on or safety off, with the gun with the activated safety, you can simply flip the safety on during tactical movement and not be required to decock or go back to that long DA trigger. Remember what the FBI said? Double action is for holding suspects and after the first shot you are in a fight and need the single action accuracy! I prefer this action, which many call Selective Double Action. Both the double action man and the single action man will be happy.

The H and K is well made and reliable above all. It is hard to compare it to the Glock, neither have malfunctioned in my hands. The H and K feels better and handles better. The Glock has only one trigger action to learn, the H and K in DA form has two. Occasionally, certain grip styles will actuate the H and K safety and place it 'on' during a firing string, but this can be addressed in training.

The H and K is accurate enough for any reasonable problem solving exercise, has good sights, and uses good cartridges. The grip frame fits most hands well, even in .45 ACP. I am split between this gun and the SW 99 as the top of the line polymer frame weapon. I prefer the handling and accuracy of the SW 99 but the H and K has a manual safety, which I strongly recommend on any combat autoloader. The H and K is a good gun that will not limit the best shooter.

Fired   50 rounds Black Hills 155 gr. JHP

           50 rounds Black Hills 180 gr. FMJ

10 yards (155gr.)   3.0 inches

25 yards (155gr.)   2.9 inches

#25 Smith and Wesson SW 99

This is a variant of the Walther P 99, but a superior one in my opinion. The SW 99 is worth choosing simply for the superior slide design.

I am very enthusiastic concerning the SW 99. In my opinion this pistol is truly a modern pistol, offering excellent handling characteristics, good accuracy, top notch reliability and more than a little flash. The pistol is a true double action first shot pistol, but the DA pull is smooth, light, and short.

The author has tremendous enthusiasm and respect for the SW 99 Smith and Wesson

The single action trigger compression is easily managed. The pistol features several grip inserts that allow it to be used by any hand size.

I tried all three, none were bad but the medium sized grip frame insert worked best for me. The pistol has a rail in the frame for use with a dedicated light and can be ordered with night sights. The sights are excellent. Overall, a great modern pistol that is largely not acclaimed. The pistol is light and compact, despite the fact that I fired the full size version. I have never fired a 'ultra modern' that I can use better than this one. Yet, it is light on the hip and easy to carry. This is a world class pistol.

Fired   100 rounds,   Federal Classic 155 grain JHP
10 yards   3.5 inches   25 yards   2.0 inches

#26 SIG P 226 9mm

As we move to the immensely popular SIG pistols, a bit of discussion is warranted. These pistols are noted for high quality, reliability, and accuracy. As for reliability there is no question. The weapons are well fitted and often among the most accurate handguns tested. They were originally designed to give life saving accuracy as needed in hostage rescue. They can deliver. These pistols have no safety, only a long double action first shot seen as a safety feature. They are among the first pistols to feature a positive firing pin block or drop safety, making them completely safe to carry chamber loaded. The double action trigger is long but often smooth. SIG makes a double action only pistol for police work that is fairly manageable but need not concern the civilian shooter. The trigger reset of the SIG is a bit slower than some pistols, but this means when you fire a rapid fire string each shot will be deliberate. The standard double action pistol is as quite acceptable for combat work, and very accurate in the single action mode. Not in mechanical terms of course, but in practical terms.

The SIG has a high bore axis that means the pistol has more muzzle flip than competing designs. The grip of the pistol is not overlarge, even in high capacity versions, and the P 220 single column grip frame downright comfortable. Some shooters affect a grip that results in the magazine release being held down when the gun fires, preventing the gun from locking open on the last round. This can be difficult to address with some hand sizes. Few pistols can match the SIG's accuracy, but on a realistic combat course that stresses control and speed shooting, a Glock or Beretta will give a better showing, given shooters of similar skill.

The pistol has trade-offs, but reliability and accuracy are there. We can work with the rest.

The P 226 9mm is a product of US Army pistol trials. This pistol tied the Beretta overall but Beretta won on the low bid. The P 226 I tested

The SIG P 226 has excelled in numerous military test programs.

was fitted with adjustable sights and was well used. It probably had 10,000 rounds on the frame and slide. It felt good in the hand and shot well enough once the double action pull was mastered. Accuracy was outstanding in the bench rest section, but when the double action first trigger compression is taken into consideration, rapid fire was not as impressive.

Fired   50 rounds, Hornady Custom 115 gr. XTP
             50 rounds, Winchester 124 grain Partition
10 yards   4.8inches
25 yards (XTP load)   1.9inches

#27 SIG P 220

This is a pistol I carried in uniform for the Duncan SC P.D. when restricted to 'any quality double action pistol.' I had been issued the SIG P 226 and found it an acceptable pistol. (I loaded mine with Cor Bon 115 grain JHP ammunition.) I purchased my own P 220. So, I had a .45 caliber double action service gun. I was confident in the pistol, but found that most .45 caliber ammunition lost about 50 to 70 fps in the short P 220 barrel. As an example, the Winchester SXT drops from 860 fps in a five inch 1911 to 780 fps from the four and one quarter inch P 220 barrel. Winchester developed the 230 gr. SXT +P for just that reason, to bring the 230 grain JHP back up to specification when fired in a SIG or Colt Commander. The P 220 has a harder push than the 1911 but is not uncomfortable. The sights were too low and small in original versions but are much improved in current production. My tired old gun shoots very well.

Fired   50 rounds Hornady 200 grain XTP +P
         50 rounds Speer 230 grain Gold Dot
10 yards   4.8 inches   25 yards (Gold Dot)   15/16 inch

The accuracy group is the best fired with any handgun and incredibly accurate for a production pistol.

#28 P 220, .38 Super

This is a thoroughly modern pistol with many good attributes. This is one of the few new out of the box pistols tested. Handling was identical to the .45 ACP but recoil much less. The problem of velocity loss is far less drastic with the .38 Super- Cor Bon 115 grain loads clocked well over 1400 fps, losing little to a five inch 1911. Accuracy was excellent. Cor Bon is the only company loading the Super to it's full potential. If you wish to own a top flight SIG and favor the comfortable P 220 grip, but do not like .45 recoil, this is the gun for you.. You have one more round and a cartridge that virtually equals the .357 Magnum.

Fired   100 rounds, Cor Bon 115 grain JHP
10 Yards   4.0 inches   25 yards   2.5 inches

#29 SIG P 228

After the Beretta 92 9mm was found to be a bit large for soldiers with small hands and for those in CID needing to conceal a handgun, the P 228 was given a rigorous test and adopted as the M 11 pistol. The P 228 as we know it is a good handgun, well balanced, accurate, and quick into action. I like it better than the P 226. It is just as accurate on average but quicker

The P 228/M11

into action and easier to handle. It is a good double action 9mm.

Fired   100 rounds Hornady 147 grain XTP

10 Yards   4.5 inches   25 yards   2.4 inches

#30 Beretta 92 9mm

The Beretta 92 has been in use by the US Army for more than twenty years as of this writing. Maintenance and reliability issues have shown the design is good. There were early problems and reports of failure that have never been properly explained, but in general use the pistol has fared well. It has a large grip frame that is a stretch for some hands, but I have seen many female shooters manage the Beretta well. The trigger action is long but smooth and the single action trigger usually good. The sights are better than either the SIG or the Glock. The pistol has a positive safety, which gives it far more consideration than the other two in my estimation. Of the three popular European produced police service pistols, I favor the Beretta over either the Glock or the SIG. The Beretta is almost never involved in an accidental discharge. Safety is between the ears but this pistol has an enviable record. The pistol features straight line feed, making it capable of feeding hollowpoints readily. The Model 92 is bulky but not heavy. Muzzle flip is not apparent- this is an easy pistol to keep on target in rapid fire strings. For a heavy duty double action 9mm, this is my first choice.

Fired   100 rounds Black Hills 115 grain JHP
Ten Yards   3.5 inches   25 yards   3.0 inches

#31 Beretta Elite

This is a top end Beretta with several good features. The pistol is fitted with Novak sights, a great improvement. The slide is redesigned for greater strength, and the grip frame modestly changed. The result is a pistol that fits the hand better, and hit potential is better with the Novak sights. The barrel is slightly shorter than the 92 version, giving a trimmer better balanced appearance. The Elite is a decocker only, which means that there is no manual safety. The safety is used only to decock the pistol. I am not sure how I feel about this. I will note that a number of competitors use the Beretta in IDPA, where the gun is required to be holstered safety on. The gun can be safely carried safety off, but those are the rules, and I have seen quite a few fumbles. A slide mounted safety will never be as fast as a frame mounted safety. So, while I like a handgun with a manual safety here we have a Beretta with SIG like features--it has safety features, not a manual safety. Overall, the Beretta Elite II is an even more impressive pistol than the original Model 92. The test gun is a 9mm. The Elite II is also available in .40 caliber. The .40 caliber version should be as pleasant to fire, given the Beretta's design and low muzzle whip. I am not easily impressed but find the Elite II something of a wonder. It builds upon solid ground but stretches the '92's performance considerably.

Fired   100 rounds, Cor Bon 124 grain JHP

10 Yards   3.8 inches   25 yards   2.0 inches

#32 Smith and Wesson 3913

Smith and Wesson has built thousands of these guns but you seldom see a used one for sale. I know why. The gun is very, very smooth, accurate, and shoots all out of proportion to it's size. This pistol features an ambidextrous manual safety, a magazine safety that prevents the gun from firing if the magazine is removed, and excellent Novak sights. Some claim the 3913 is more accurate than the full size Smith

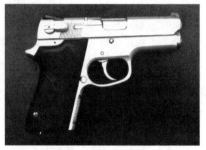

Trim, attractive and capable - the 3913

and Wesson pistols. This may be, but I cannot prove it. I do not use a machine rest, preferring to keep in touch with reality. The action of my gun is smooth, and the frame features serrations in the right spot to aid in control. Hogue rubber grips round out the features. This pistol is on 3,500 trouble free rounds. This pistol is just the right size, well made of good material, and offers practical safety features that are much appreciated. It is a sophisticated weapon that will serve anyone well.

Fired   50 rounds Hornady 115 gr. XTP

          50 rounds Black Hills 115 gr. +P

10 yards   4.0 inches   25 yards (Hornady)   2.5 inches

#33 Colt 1991A1

As we begin to examine the 1911 type pistols, I am certain we will meet with controversy. Some love the 1911, some hate it. There are many who are interested in revisionist history for

reasons of their own and attempt to discount the incredible performance of the 1911 pistol and it's formidable cartridge. The truth is not in question. Military after action reports and congressional records detailing the exploits of Medal of Honor winners speak highly of the 1911. Suggestions to the

The Colt 1911 .45 and the .38 Smith and Wesson Cheif's Special make an excellent combination

contrary, especially those concerning the veracity of our fighting men, are not well taken. We have even seen the exploits of Sgt. York taken to task in print. I can only say that no one would have taken such drivel to his face when he lived! And, frankly, while Sgt. York's feat at arms was tremendous, shooting and stopping seven armed men with a pistol, it is not unique.

The 1911 type pistol has a low bore axis which limits muzzle flip. The single action, straight to the rear trigger compression makes for excellent control and accuracy. The pistol fits most hands well. The side lock safety, grip safety, and disconnector, as well as the positive firing pin block in modern pistols, makes for an intrinsically safe handgun. Just the same, the 1911 is not for everyone. Extensive training and monthly practice, weekly is preferred-are required to get the most of this pistol, to master this formidable weapon. There is no other weapon that can serve as well as the 1911. No other type has dominated competition they way the 1911 has. Combat is not competition, but the 1911 is a true all around handgun. It is even suitable for taking medium game at moderate range. It would be foolish indeed to hunt whitetail deer with the 9mm, but I have taken several with the .45 ACP. Here is a pistol we can bet our lives on in confidence. The 1911 is not perfect-it requires lubrication to maintain it's reliability, while some modern types need almost no oil or grease. It is a bit heavy for daily wear, but the Commander solves that problem.

The 1991A1 is a Government Model designed to sell at a reduced price. The pistol has a matte finish, which is less labor intensive, and is supplied with inexpensive rubber grips. But internally, it is all Colt. I have owned several and fired dozens. The 1991A1 is reliable, feeds hollowpoints, and shares the virtues of the 1911 tribe. It will not perform as well as a fifteen hundred dollar custom gun in terms of accuracy, trigger compression, and other details, but it is reliable and accurate enough for any reasonable purpose. That is all we can ask.

Rounds fired   100 Federal American Eagle 230 gr. Ball
10 yards   4.0 inches   25 yards   3.9 inches

#34 Para Ordnance LDA 7.45

This is the compact version of the LDA series. Here we find a weapon of obvious high quality, with a spotless, well finished exterior and no tool marks to be found. The gun is very smooth, has excellent sights, and offers first rate reliability. The action is a Light

Superior in every way, the Para Ordnance 7.45 LDA

Double Action. The gun is fired by a single long pull of the trigger which cocks and fires the weapon. With each shot, the slide recoils but unlike single action pistols the hammer is not cocked, but rides down with the slide. The slide lock safety and grip safety operate in the normal manner, and it is recommended the LDA is carried on safe. Like all 1911s, the safety is easily manipulated due to it's perfectly located position. The LDA is surprisingly accurate and easy to use well. Some shooters clutch the light trigger of the 1911, and will jerk a shot with a four pound trigger. The LDA breaks at about six pounds of compression but feels lighter. The gun is far more compact than the SIG, Glock or Smith and Wesson double actions and offers a superior safety system to any other handgun, without exception. It has only one trigger action to master, and features a positive safety. There is no better personal defense weapon than the 7.45 and no better service weapons than the full size Para Ordnance pistols.

Fired   50 rounds Hornady 230 grain ball
           50 rounds Cor Bon 165 grain JHP

10 yards   3.6 inches   25 yards (Hornady) 3.5 inches

#35 Colt Commander

This is my personal Commander. I fitted a Wilson Combat front

strap cover which gives the feel of custom checkering without the cost, and also Wilson Combat grips after much experimentation with other types.

This gun came out of the box shooting and has never failed. Modern 1911s seem free from the break in malfunctions once associated with the

An American icon, a name to conjure with - the Colt Commander

type. This pistol has adequate if not outstanding sights, and is available in stainless steel finish, the first choice for hard use. I like this gun very much.

It is far from the most accurate 1911 off the bench, but it comes into the hand quickly and does the business like no other. The short sight radius is good for short range 'nitty gritty' shooting as my friend and combat veteran Sid Hawkins tells us.

Fired   100 rounds Triton 185 grain JHP +P

10 Yards   4.0 inches   25 yards   3.0 inches

#36 High Standard G Man

This is a pistol I have carried and used for several years, firing some 10,000 rounds in the process. I now have Wilson Combat night sights fitted, and an Armor Tuff Wilson Combat finish on the slide. The G Man is fitted with the Safety Fast Shooting system. This system allows the hammer to be carried down but the gun instantly ready for a single action shot. Cock the gun, press the ham-

mer forward and the safety springs on. Release the safety and the hammer flies to the rear. This is accomplished by an internal hammer which is cocked when the external part of the two piece hammer is lowered. The SFS is an option with the High Standard. This allows those not comfortable with cocked and locked carry, or whose chiefs, mayors, or administrators are not willing to accept cocked and locked carry, to deploy with a 1911. The LDA is an option to the same problem but Cylinder and Slide Shop, Inc, can fit the SFS to an exist-

The High Standard was very effective in rapid fire against this Gibson steel target

ing gun. It is rugged and the High Standard has maintained a crisp 3.5 pound trigger compression through all of the firing I have done. I respect this handgun very much. It is a top notch handgun from a progressive company.

Fired   100 Federal 230 grain Hydra Shock

10 yards   3.6 inches   25 yards   1.25 inch

#37 Colt Government Model

I was surprised by this gun. I found it new in the box at a good price, and it is not a high end Colt but one of several variants made up about the time Colonel Keyes took over the helm of Colt. He demanded and got quality production. The pistol has the standard Government Model sights, forward cocking serrations, an aluminum trigger with a de-

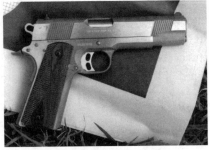

When all is said and done, Colt maintains tremendous name recognition and remains a fine product

cent break, and very nice checkered wooden grips. This is a first class pistol offered at a fair price.

Fired   50 Speer 200 grain Gold Dot +P
         50 Federal 185 grain JHP

10 yards	4.5 inches	25 yards	3.25 inches

#38 Kimber Custom II

My example was ordered in blue finish. I asked Dwight van Brunt of Kimber to send a base gun, the least expensive Kimber of all as my test gun. There are Kimbers with more features, such as adjustable sights, stainless construction, night sights and front strap checkering but none are better fitted or more reliable. I have a lot of time in with the Kimber line and find a respectable pistol offered at a fair price. I can't say this is the best 1911 available but I cannot recommend any other 1911 over the Kimber. To procure a better weapon would demand a considerable expenditure over the Kimber's price. Over the years, we have come to realize that 1911 performance relies upon hand fitting. Some guns are better than others, even in Colt production of such excellent lines as the old Series 70. I never saw a bad Series 70 but some were much better than others. No maker of 1911s was immune to this. Some guns required longer break ins and the trigger compression could run from five to eight pounds. Not so with the Kimber. These pistols are as consistent as the SIG, which is saying a great deal. Almost any Kimber trigger I applied my RCBS trigger pull gauge to compressed and broke at 4 1/4 pounds, with very little deviation. Knowing my way around the 1911 and having built quite a few, this is impressive. When you rack the slide of the Kimber, the locking lugs and barrel bushing feel right, the link is never too long or too short. The guns feed any good ammunition and accuracy is of a high order, as long as the shooter does his part. The slide lock safety and grip safety operate exactly as they should. Recently, the LAPD SWAT team adopted the Kimber as standard issue, with certain refinements. I have examined a number of pistols that cost twice as much as the Kimber, including the FBI SWAT team pistol. It would be difficult indeed to justify the purchase of such a pistol when the Kimber is available and offers such a high order of performance. This is the gun that those who imitate Colt have failed to build.

Fired 100 Black Hills 230 grain JHP

10 Yards	3.4 inches	25 yards	2.1 inches

#39 Kimber Compact

There was a long and arduous journey in producing a compact 1911 that is reliable. The barrel bushing had to be done away with and a coned barrel designed. This allows the slide to run further to the rear in recoil, insuring proper function. The coned barrel locks up as tight as the barrel bushing. The full length guide rod was designed to keep the recoil spring from kinking in compact pistols. After some time and evaluation, I avoided small 1911s for reliability reasons. After all, my life was literally on the line. Now, there are a number of small 1911s that are good performers. The stainless compact Kimber illustrated has fired thousands of rounds without any problem. As long as you hold the sights properly on target and squeeze the trigger, the gun will give you a hit. Of course it is more difficult to use well than a full size 1911, but it is a fine concealed carry weapon. And it is practically as accurate as many full sized pistols from a solid rest.

Fired 100 rounds Fiocchi 230 grain ball

10 Yards	4.9 inches	25 yards	2.9 inches

#40 Kimber Pro Carry

This is a new idiom in the 1911 tribe. The pistol features a full length grip frame. In other words, it holds a seven shot magazine, same as the Government Model and Commander. The 7.45, Compact, and Officer's Model 1911s have smaller frames and a six shot magazine. But the Pro Carry has a longer slide than the Officer's Model, but shorter than the Commander.

The Kimber Pro Carry is a different sort of 1911 but one well appreciated by all who own it.

The Pro Carry features a four inch barrel. I was not sure I would like this size pistol, but what's not to like? The pistol has excellent sights, a good trigger, and feels right in the hand. The four inch barrel clears leather quickly as we demonstrated several times on the range. The pistol is genuinely well balanced. This gun cost more than the Commander and similar guns, but it has better sights, a better trigger, and is overall well put together. I prefer the full size Custom II for all around use, but I am a hunter and sport shooter as well as a defensive hand gunner. For a pure carry gun, the Pro Carry is an outstanding choice.

Fired   100 Cor Bon 230 grain JHP

10 yards   4.0inches   25 yards   1.8 inches

#41 Kimber Target Model, .38 Super

Years ago, we often remarked that adjustable sights have no place on a combat handgun. Considering what was available at the time, this was a correct perception. The adjustable sights offered on this handgun are rugged enough for the hardest chores. The adjustments are repeatable and exact. The pistol is all Kimber, that is, an outstanding handgun in all regards. But the sights give a more exact sight picture than the standard fixed sight Kimbers. Don't get me wrong, the fixed sights on the Custom II are as good as they come. But the rear notch in the Kimber adjustable sights is smaller, allowing more precise fire at the cost of a little speed. The .38 Super is for all practical defense purposes in the .357 Magnum range, given proper ammunition. There is only one company offering ammunition loaded to the full potential of the Super, and that is Cor Bon. The 115 grain bullet breaks well over 1,400 fps in the Kimber and the 125 grain JHP about 1,350 fps. The Kimber makes the most of either. With two more shots than the .45, better penetration, and lighter recoil, this is a weapon to conjure with.

Fired   50 Cor Bon 115 gr. JHP

          50 Cor Bon 124 gr. JHP

10 yards   2.9 inches   25 yards   1.5 inches

#42 Wilson Combat Close Quarters Battle

The CQB is not Wilson's top of the line pistol but it is a very good one and among the best buys in top end 1911s, pistols that are around two thousand dollars in price. The pistol features excellent fit

The Wilson Combat makes top grade tactical pistols

and finish, the top of the line Wilson Combat safety, grip safety, and sights, and a very nice trigger compression of about 3.5 pounds. The magazine well features an effective but low profile magazine funnel, and the grips are well designed for good purchase. This is the 1911 you will go to when you find you have outgrown the more common fare.

Fired   50 rounds Wilson Combat 200 gr. XTP

50 rounds Hornady 185 gr. XTP

10 yards   2.8 inches   25 yards (Hornady)   1.65inches

#43 Armscor Medallion

I have used several Philippine produced 1911s with excellent luck. The ones that bear the Rock Island Arsenal name have been good solid GI type guns, in both .38 Super and .45 auto. They are inexpensive but well made. I have also examined a number of others, from different importers, that did not work as well. The Medallion is an improved version of the Armscor line with excellent features, including one of the first true slide redesigns in 1911 history. The pistol feature front serrations, an excellent adjustable sight, a well designed ambidextrous safety,

The Medallion offers a host of good features and solid performance

and Pachmayr grips. Many parts of the Medallion, including the grip safety and mainspring housing, are finely checkered. The pistol's trigger compression is 3.5 pounds and it feeds all hollowpoints. Accuracy is good. This is as good a gun as can be had for the price, about six hundred dollars. So far so good, this gun bears watching. Looks are not everything, but after all of the time I have spent with the 1911 I find I like the Medallion's looks a lot.

Fired   50 Federal 185 grain Hydra Shock +P

10 yards   3.8 inches   25 yards, 230 gr. Load 3.1 inches.

#44 Smith and Wesson 457 .45 Auto

Here is a gun that is not quite in the league with the 3913 in fit and appearance, but a very good shooter. The 457 is a member of Smith and Wesson's value line. This means the gun is not as well polished or blued as other guns, and the sights are not Novaks, in fact they are plastic. The safety is right hand only instead of ambidextrous. The pistols are sold at quite a discount over the four digit guns but seem to work well. After all, the lockwork and construction are the same but labor intensive polishing and certain expensive amenities are deleted. The 457 is a compact pistol just a bit larger than the 3913 Smith and Wesson 9mm. This pistol features a double action first shot, a positive slide mounted safety, and good reliability. My personal example has been customized by Actions by T. The action is very, very smooth. In stock form, it was usable. After Teddy's Action job the pistol is not more accurate intrinsically, but in practical off hand shooting the gun is much easier to use well. I do not like to compare pistols against the other as many have positive merits, and of course the more expensive pistols are usually better performers than less expensive pistols, as may be expected. But I cannot help but compare the 457 to the SIG P245 compact. The SIG cost almost twice as much as the Smith and Wesson. The Smith and Wesson offers basically the same performance but has the addition of a manual safety than you can use or disregard. The Smith and Wesson has less muzzle flip and can be brought to a different level of smoothness in the trigger action at relatively small expense. The SIG may be more trendy but the 457 is the better performer overall, regardless of price.

Fired   50 Winchester USA 230 gr. Ball

           50 Winchester 230 gr. SXT

10 yards   5.0inches   25 yards (USA ball) 2.9 inches

#45 FM High Power

I am fully aware that many of us are on a strict budget. Braces, cheerleader outfits, summer camp and college takes precedence over the Custom Special .45. Some of us simply wish to own a good solid weapon that will not break the bank. The Taurus revolvers I previously covered clearly fit that fill, as do the Smith and Wesson value line handguns. An exceptional handgun I have had good results with is the FM High Power, a clone of the 1911 manufactured in Argentina. I am up to a dozen and three custom FM pistols in my experience, all with fine results.
The most recent guns have good combat safeties, but in the past I simply added the reasonably priced unit from Cylinder and Slide Shop, Inc. The FM is the best clone gun of the High Power I have fired. It is not as

Proven and world-class, the 5906 Sith and Wesson

nicely finished as the true Browning, and the trigger is heavier, but it costs half what the Browning cost. Low cost is often a warning but the FM High Power, as imported by the Dealer Warehouse, works. Here is a quality 9mm that won't break the bank and offers a usable defensive handgun that will not put anyone at a disadvantage. The latest example I tested had a decent trigger action, breaking at five pounds with a bit of creep. Overall, a good single action 9mm capable of depending home and hearth.

Fired   100 rounds Black Hills 147 grain JHP

10 Yards	3.6 inches	25 yards	4.25 inches

#46 Smith and Wesson 5906

This is one of the finest modern 9mm Luger pistols, bar none. The Third Generation pistols were introduced to meet the challenge of the SIG pistol. They have more than equaled their competitor. The 5906 features stainless steel construction, a positive safety, a firing pin safety and magazine safety, and excellent reliability and accuracy. The safety system, both the manual safety and the magazine safety, has saved the lives of many peace officers. The only way I could tell you about this would be to borrow heavily from the work of Captain Massad Ayoob. The good Captain has documented many cases of on safe carry defeating a gun grab attempt. He has also documented a case in which the officer managed to hit the magazine release, bringing the magazine safety into play, thereby rendering the pistol incapable of firing. I am not certain all criminals would be so dumb, but I have yet to meet a street punk who was a mental giant. Still, there have been ex cops and ex soldiers up to mayhem and they may well be able to actuate the safety quickly. But history and the opinion of many martial artists points to the 5906 being among the best choices in all around tactical efficiency. Only the Browning High Powers shares the Smith and Wesson's manual safety and magazine safety, to the best of my knowledge. (The JP Sauer double action pocket pistol that is the ancestor of the modern SIG also shared these attributes.) If you are of the mind that these are tactical advantages, the 5906 is the gun for you. Those who favor a simpler system will go to another handgun. I borrowed a pistol from our local police department to conduct this firing test and the pistol was pulled from a rack and handed over. Performance was good, as was expected.

Ammunition fired 100 rounds Hornady 124 grain ball

10 Yards	3.5 inches	25 yards	2.5 inches

#47 Taurus PT 92

The PT 92 is a clone of the 1970s version of the Beretta 92. At the time, the Beretta was the standard military firearm of the Brazilian armed forces. When the military contract expired, Taurus bought the machinery that had been set up in Brazil. The original Model 92 featured a slide lock safety, much like the Browning High Power. Police authorities in Europe asked that the Beretta be redesigned with a decocker, and Beretta responded with the slide mounted safety and decocker we are all so familiar with. The original was not a bad system and tactically superior in many ways. Selective double action is a popular system with many professionals. The Taurus has found favor with several trainers who appreciate the fact that the pistol can be used to train shooters to manipulate either double action or single action systems. The Taurus is not as well finished as the Beretta, at least in early versions, but is usually reliable. It will not feed hollowpoints as well as modern Beretta production. The Beretta has been considerably improved while the Taurus 92 is stuck in a time warp. However, I like the pistol. When it is fed loads that function well and feed properly, such as the Winchester Silvertip, the pistol is

reliable. It can be carried cocked and locked, hammer down and safety on, or hammer down and safety off, all safely. Many shooters buy the Taurus as a second gun or car gun due to it's affordable price.   Modern production is better finished and fitted and the price has crept

With few reservations, the Taurus 92 gave good service

up accordingly. New production pistols have one problem that is not easily addressed. Taurus has received few police contracts due to the lack of a decocker. Yet, the pistol has been praised due to it's frame mounted safety. The frame mounted safety is quickly actuated and easy to reach well, far easier than the Beretta safety.   Taurus engineers managed to incorporate a decocker into this safety. A hard push downwards on the safety decocks the hammer. The problem is, this can occur when the gun is being fired. It has happened to me on numerous occasions when test firing various '92s and PT 100s. With some shooters, it happens with almost every shot. You have to consciously train yourself to keep you thumb straight along the grip, not riding on the safety. This is for the following reason. When you thumb the safety off the natural inclination is to leave the thumb on the safety and let it ride there during firing. If you do, the gun will decock during the firing string. For 1911 shooters especially, who nearly always ride the grip safety when firing, the 92 safety is a challenge. This is a shame as the pistol is a decent handgun. The best solution is to buy a set of Pachmayr grips for the old type Taurus. These grips do not allow the safety to move to the decock position. The new model grips hurt nothing on the old gun, as the cut out is simply non functional, but the old style grips serve a real purpose on the new gun-blocking the decocker. This is not exactly the liability threatening act of deactivating a safety, but an expedient necessary to allow the use of this handgun. So, we have a pistol that is far more nicely finished in new production and feeds hollowpoints better but has a serious defect in the safety system. Purchase grips designed for the older gun, and be certain they do not have the decocker cut out, and you have a gun faithful to the original template. Before you discount this safety as old fashioned, remember that Beretta offers a special tactical version of the Model 92 that offers guess what? A manual safety offering cocked and locked carry! The Beretta Tactical is far more expensive than the Taurus. What does the Taurus really offer other than the safety system? A gun that is comfortable to fire, with little muzzle flip, a good magazine capacity, and a comfortable grip.

Fired   100 rounds Black Hills 124 grain FMJ

10 yards	2.5 inches	Single action
	4.5 inches	First shot double action
25 yards	3.5 inches	

#48 Smith and Wesson 3953

This is the double action only version of the 3913. Since it is used by several agencies including the plainclothes officers of the Royal Canadian Mounted Police, I though it worth looking at . A

reason for adoption of the pistol by the RCMP was that transition from the revolver was much easier.

The pistol has a longer grip frame in the rear than the 3913, which dampens recoil comfortably. The trigger breaks at about ten pounds, with a normal at rest position midway between the double action and single action trigger of the 3913. I found it fairly easy to use well with acclimation, but in firing for accuracy the DAO trigger was a challenge. It is not revolver smooth but will do for short range de-

The Smith and Wesson DAO pistols simply did not perform as well in shooting tests as the other action types tested

fense. The RCMP has men who managed to shoot the full size DAO 5946 (A DAO 5906) well to fifty yards. I am not one of these. For most of us, DAO remains a difficult trigger action to master.

Fired   50 rounds Winchester USA 124 grain ball
              50 rounds Cor Bon 115 gr. JHP
10 yards (Cor Bon)   6.0 inches
25 yards (Winchester)   5.5 inches

#49 Smith and Wesson SIGMA

The SIGMA is Smith and Wesson's answer to the Glock. The pistol features a polymer frame and a long double action only trigger. The SIGMA is reliable, but that is the only praise I can give this gun. Well, it does fit most hands well. I understand that Smith and Wesson needed a gun to compete with Glock. If someone was convinced that DAO and polymer was the wave of the future, the 5906 will not sway them. The SIGMA is the most difficult of all the DAO polymer frame pistols to shoot well. I simply do not like the action, and have found not a single professional who carries the gun on his own time, of his own choice.

Fired   100 rounds Black Hills 180 grain JHP
10 Yards   5.0 inches   25 yards   6.5 inches

#50 Ceiner conversion unit

This unit practically deserves it's own chapter. Many companies offer .22 caliber conversion units for the Colt. Wilson Combat and Kimber offer top notch units - and so does Ceiner. But Ceiner also offers .22 caliber units for the Beretta and the AR 15 among other firearms.

We all need a good .22 and when that .22 is our service gun, practice is especially relevant

Simply remove the slide assembly of the Beretta and replace it with the .22 caliber slide and magazine. You are ready to go! I have perhaps 2,500 rounds in this unit, and many more trouble free rounds from the 1911 unit. These are first class units that give the shooter on a budget a good option for shooting practice.

Rounds fired	100 Winchester Wildcat		
Ten yards	2.0 inches	25 yards	1.6 inches

CHAPTER 16
THE CUSTOM OPTION

In this chapter we will look at the custom option for making a handgun perform better. To the person who is about gimmicks, this would be the most important chapter and there are books dedicated to customizing handguns. To the person who is about tactics, this chapter is not about anything he or she wishes to read. The best outlook is somewhere in the middle. For most of my life I have used custom guns of one sort or the other with complete satisfaction and utter reliability. At other times, I have seen the gun butcher ruin perfectly serviceable service guns. You cannot make a silk purse of a sow's ear and cut rate guns or guns with problems simply cannot be made as reliable or accurate as a top quality handgun. But if you begin with quality, you can end up with a handgun that will perform beyond your expectations. I am a firm believer in what is needed and nothing more in a service or personal defense handgun. Much of what we see used in competition is counter productive to personal defense. Sure, good sights are an asset but only if they are top grade high visibility, not necessarily adjustable, sights.

Extended magazine buttons and extended slide locks, often fitted to competition handguns, can produce serious problems on the street. An extended magazine release can dump your magazine when you need it or even bump the magazine loose in the holster. An extended slide stop can tie up with a touch during a firing string. On the other hand, a larger but not excessive slide lock safety on a 1911 can make for better combat ability.

When we discuss custom handguns, most of us think of the 1911 type pistol. Just mention the 1911 and you can find yourself in a rancorous debate, a brawl with linguistic bludgeons. People have strong feelings on both sides of the debate. The 1911 is, in my opinion, a model of ergonomic perfection. Others find it over complicated. High magazine capacity is important to some doctrines, and the 1911 is not a high magazine capacity handgun. In fact, none of my personal defense handguns are! My argument may be that no gun is too big to fight with while others will refrain you cannot have enough ammunition. So many factors come into play the debate can be difficult indeed and will never be resolved. But I do think we can all agree that no handgun comes from the factory perfect for each shooter.

I have enjoyed custom 1911 pistols from several of the top pistol smiths in the country. I have also shot and used custom SIG and Beretta pistols, as well as a revolver, from a man who specializes in action work. He is very good at what he does. Teddy Jacobsen of Sugarland, Texas focuses on reliability above all else. And now we get to the truly important aspects of custom work and handgun modification. Ask yourself, does your handgun ever misfire, is it as reliable as you would like? Only by practice and handling the weapon will you answer this question. Even the most reliable factory handguns can benefit from a careful attention to the barrel, chamber, feed ramp, and magazine. Teddy is a master of this work.

The action of the handgun is another matter. There are two types of accuracy, intrinsic and practical. If you bolt the handgun into a machine rest, there are a number of modern types that will fire five rounds of quality ammunition into perhaps four inches at fifty yards. But if the trigger action is stiff, long, full of creep, or has excessive backlash, you will never be able to accomplish this type of shooting off hand. Personal defense shooting is about off hand shooting. I could care less what my pistol will do from a bench rest. If it has a lousy trigger, poor sights and a sharp edged grip frame, I will never be able to use it well off hand. When you have action work done that makes the trigger compression smoother-not necessarily lighter, but smoother-you have affected the intrinsic accuracy of the weapon not a whit. But the practical accuracy will be much improved.

Teddy Jacobsen can take a revolver or semi auto and make the trigger action much more usable. As an example, after his action work on a Beretta pistol the long double action stroke was not nearly as offensive because it was much smoother than before. I also enjoy a bobbed hammer Taurus 85 revolver that Teddy performed an action job on. While the bobbed hammer is a necessity for deep concealment, this snag free revolver gives up the single action option. After Teddy carefully worked the action, I hardly miss single action fire. The double action trigger is that good.

Another option that Teddy performs is to shave the grips of the Beretta 92, giving them an ultra modern appearance and making the pistol just a bit slimmer for those with small hands. With the action job and grip slimming as a combination, the Beretta is a transformed pistol. Just a little adds up to a lot!

Teddy has also performed a great deal of work on Glock handguns. Teddy warns us there is not lot that can be safely done with a Glock trigger, but he can make reset and take up tighter.

If you wish to go a bit further with your 1911 Don Williams of the Acton Works offers Serious Guns for Serious Times, as his motto. Some time ago, as a jaded 1911 man, I wished to build up a Browning High Power similar to the one used by the FBI HRT at the time. Don fitted a set of Novak sights, front and rear, to the pistol, with considerable machine work involved. He adjusted the action to a very crisp note as well. The usual reliability package was added. Intrinsic accuracy was not addressed, but I was surprised when I field tested the weapon. I had been unable to use the High Power well due to the poor sights and trigger. At fifty yards, firing from prone position during police qualification, I fired a five shot four inch group at fifty yards, using Pro Load 124 grain JHP ammunition. The local Sheriffs's Department, using SIG P 226s, did not post nearly so perfect a fifty yard group. Impressive? You bet. But several 1911s built by the Action Works, fitted with match grade barrels and solid, match grade barrel bushings, will do the same. And they never malfunction.

Sharp edges on the frame are ruinous to clothing and will lacerate your hands if you are not careful. But makers still produce pistols with sharp edges. Don Williams offers a smooth out package that is a great aid in overall handling and comfort. Don's sight work is good, and many of his handguns are serving with armed professionals.

An important point in custom work is that older guns can be upgraded with new parts and refreshed. As an example, my old 669 Smith and Wesson compact was state of the art in it's day but the third generation Smith and Wessons were much better in terms of trigger action and feel.

Teddy Jacobsen performed an outstanding action job on this gun. This was my first experience with his shop. After the work, the gun was as smooth as any new gun, including anything SIG or Smith and Wesson had to offer.

A set of small compact Pachmayr grips and the gun was complete. Years later, virtually the same work was done with a Model 457 .45 auto.

Changing the grips or finish of a handgun is simply personalization. Installing custom sights and performing action work is true custom work. A balky gun has to be repaired and improved or discarded, but a good gun can be made even better by carefully chosen custom work. Good sights, a smooth action, and complete reliability are our goal. The guns illustrated meet that criteria.

CHAPTER 17
WHAT IFS AND CONTROVERSY

It is easy to box yourself into a hole when designing tactical scenarios. You can overstretch the capabilities of both gun and shooter easily. Multiple targets, long range problems, and problems of speed can outpace the shooter's performance rather quickly. But any drill we undertake on the range should be grounded in reality. In most critical incidents the marksmanship problem is not severe. The problem of calming your nerves and keeping a cool head is another thing. Just the same, there are a number of nagging problems that crop up every so often. Just when you think a false precept is buried, someone comes along and reinvents the problem, often being quite self assured he is the first one to think this way.

We have to shoot down false assumptions and return to the basics of weapon craft, training, and serviceable weapons. I will examine the common controversies and opinions and take a hard look at either side as fairly as possible. I don't think there is any controversy as far as handgun reliability goes, it is either there or it isn't and the individual shooter can verify that. The caliber controversy is simply common sense. Some of the others require a little more work to prove or disprove and in the end it's personal preference. Bad training has been responsible for quite a number of legal woes, hardship and even deaths. Use common sense when approaching this problem. As an example, a systematic training system somehow was instituted in a major agency. The main point of the system was to hold a person at gunpoint when handcuffing them; bad conduct in my opinion. I have arrested dozens of non violent offenders and would have been wrong and perhaps cowardly to have held each one at gunpoint. I have taken felons at gunpoint but they were few and dangerous. This agency had recruits practice placing the gun in the hollow of the person's back they were handcuffing. If the person moved, 'feedback' would be felt in the gun hand! Pre-

dictably, there were backshots of non violent persons and big
pay offs. I have felt feedback and tenseness in a person's arms
and applied more pressure to keep them stabilized and also been
more ready for an attack-but sometimes it was simply the stress
of an arrest for a stupid or drunken mistake. This situation was
rectified and everyone commented on how absurd the training
program was, but no one had the foresight to see the results before some one was injured.

In other cases, trainers have strived to be different, perhaps for ego reasons or in the hope of taking their own path. The
basics became the basics because they work. I have seen an
alternate to the Weaver stance called the Axis Lock or something like that. I looks like a gangster thing and blocks the vision as the arms and gun are held high beside the head. Ernest
Hemingway once said that we must master the basic forms of
writing before we experiment with the English language. The
same is true of tactical groundwork. Master the basics completely and then strive for a higher goal, but to be different is
sometimes to be wrong.

I have also seen a tactic promulgated in which the weak
hand thumb is used to address the magazine release of the combat handgun. This brings forth a host of questions. The handgun
is the one hand gun and what if the weak hand is injured? At one
time I subscribed to the rapid, sure movement of simply grasp-
ing the rear of the slide after reloading and releasing the slide,
loading the gun. After due thought, I practiced the more difficult drill of thumbing the slide lock after a speed load. (I can
reload with one hand as well+ it isn't pretty and not really fast
but I can do it.)

I wondered what would happen if something happened to
my weak hand. I have trained myself to use both techniques
well. For the life of me, I can see no profit and a lot wrong using
the weak hand to address the magazine release. The weak hand
is busy with revolver reloads but should be limited to addressing
the magazine in autoloader drills.

POINT SHOOTING
Every generation someone comes along and discovers point shooting. Usually, they will manage to have an article printed on the subject and accuse the 'establishment' of ignoring point shooting and thereby costing officers their lives. And so on- point shooting or instinctive shooting does not work, at least with the handgun. Only the shotgun is aimed largely by feel and then we have a bead sight. The closest thing to point shooting that works is the Applegate drill and as you have seen the Applegate drill uses the sights. A system of body aiming that ignores the sights simply cannot work, and a system that advocates firing the handgun from below eye level past contact range must be discounted. The feats of trick shooters are just that: feats. You thought I would say tricks? No, what appears to be unaimed fire is the product of thousands, often hundreds of thousands of rounds fired in practice and some type of aiming. Of course we could do it, given normal physical strength and coordination and twenty years or so. But take a look at the fastest men alive-top end handgun competitors and the incredible Miculek, our modern revolver marvel. They use their sights. There is one argument that should quite the point shooting advocate, 'Would you like to tell a judge in a wrongful death hearing you taught your officers NOT to use their sights?'

Not me.

DOUBLE TAPS
Double taps are a harder issue to address. I originally intended to include this section in advanced tactics but after consideration felt that it should be included in this, the final chapter. The argument is basically this: some teach students to fire two shots as quickly as possible, in order to double the wound potential on the target. This is a viable concept. I am in complete agreement. It works and has worked even with minor calibers.

Others claim that if the first shot does not do the business, the second shot may not either. There is some truth to this. Several light blows do not normally carry the weight of a single heavy blow, as any boxer will tell us. But that second hit will not make the adversary feel better! Much depends upon the range, the shooter, and for once, the weapon. Some handguns, such as the 1911 and the High Power and the marvelous little Astra A 70 I often carry are controllable and exhibit very little muzzle flip. At moderate ranges a double tap is a wise choice. With a hard recoiling .357 Magnum revolver, which has a smaller ammunition reserve, perhaps a double tap would not work well.

But the real controversy is in addressing multiple targets. Multiple assailants are a rarity in numbers over two but certainly not out of the question. Addressing a triple threat with a handgun is a daunting proposition. Do we wish to double tap three targets or run each with a single round and come back to the one that did not go down? Some time ago, I conducted a test for Law Enforcement Technology to qualify the issues. I used a Colt 1911 .45 of course as the primary weapon but also used other common law enforcement weapons. The extra time needed to fire a second shot was not a consideration. Swinging between the targets at seven yards was what took our time. Firing one shot at each target was the first drill, then we fired a second run with two shots on each target and timed the results with our Competition Electronics Pocket Pro. The results? On average the run took .4 seconds longer to address three targets with two shots rather than one each. As ranges increase, more time is required to strike the target, muzzle flip is more of a problem, and the double tap less attractive. But the double tap remains a viable tactic at short range and something that should be practiced.

DISCUSSION OF DOUBLE TAPS

It is important to understand the differences in double taps. Here they are as I have been taught and practiced.These are worthy drills that can be lifesavers.

Types of double taps
The Hammer
Used at point blank range, almost at contact range.The gun

is thrust at the target and a rough sight picture taken. The trigger is pressed twice as quickly as possible. At ranges past ten feet the bullets will be widely dispersed and the second shot may miss the target all together.

The double tap

The gun is aimed and fired. As soon as the front sight is roughly in the rear sight groove a second shot is fired. Useful to about seven yards.

The controlled pair

A shot is fired with deliberation and the second shot is fired after a second, careful aim. Greater accuracy is demanded at longer ranges.

Naturally, common sense must be applied to each case. Firing two shots at every target will slow you down and result in being targeted, killed or injured. But when you can, the advantages of two shots delivered to the target are obvious. And isn't that what it is all about - common sense?

I hope the advice and fact in this book are well taken. They are the result considerable effort, research and more than a little real life stress, injury and action.

Regards,
R K Campbell

SOURCES

Actions by T
16315 Redwood Forest Court
Sugarland Texas 77478

Action Works
Don Williams
3030 Center Street West
Chino Valley Az 86323

Holsters
Alessi Holsters
2465 Niagra Falls Blvd
Amherst NY 14228

Ted Blocker
9396 Tigard
Tigard Oregon 97223

Burns Custom Pistols
(Exclusive source of several Alessi holsters)
700 Gilman Avenue #116
Issaquah WA 98027

DeSantis Holster and Leather Goods
PO 2039
New Hyde Park NY 11040

Graham's Custom Gunleather
2206 SE Hogan Rd
Gresham Oregon 97080

Don Hume Leathergoods
 PO 351

Miami Ok 74355
High Noon Holsters
PO 2138
Palm Harbor Fl 34682

Kramer Handgun Leather
PO 112154
Tacoma Wa   98411

Ken Null Holsters
163 School St NW
Resaca Ga. 30735

Milt Sparks Holsters
605 East 44th St #2
Boise Idaho 83714

Tauris Holsters
Michael Taurisano
3695 Mohawk Drive
New Hartford NY 13413

Vega Holster SRL
Industrial Area "I Moretti"
Calcinatta 56030 (PI) Italy

Wild Bill's Concealment Gunleather
PO 1941
Garner NC 27529

Politically Correct Hunting

An irreverent romp through the world of hunting, poking a little fun at hunters and a lot of fun at their animal rights opponents. Posing as an alphabetical dictionary of

hunting lore, Politically Correct Hunting dispenses jokes, tall tales and homey wisdom.

As Jim Zumbo, Editor of Outdoor Life, says: "Politically Correct Hunting is a fun book that should be on every hunter's night-stand. Ken Jacobson's wit will keep you amused, informed and entertained. This book is loaded with tips, jokes and some downright good philosophy."

Just mail in our simple-to-use form here to order copies, or call: (425) 454-7009. Mail to: Merril Press, PO Box 1682, Bellevue, WA 98009:

— — — — — — — — — — — — — — — — — — —

DISCOUNT SCHEDULE

1 COPY	$14.95	25 COPIES	$250.00
5 COPIES	$67.00	50 COPIES	$425.00
10 COPIES	$120.00	100 COPIES	$800.00

Please send me_____copies of *Politically Correct Hunting.* Enclosed is my check or money order in the amount of $_____.

Please charge my: ☐Visa ☐Mastercard ☐AMEX ☐Discover

Number: _____**Expires:** _____

Signature:_____

Print Name: _____

Street: _____

City: _____ **State:** _____ **Zip:**_____

Phone: (_____)_____

— — — — — — — — — — — — — — — — — — —

GEORGE W. BUSH
SPEAKS TO THE NATION

Since the beginning of his presidency, George W. Bush has been blowing his critics away with the power and finesse of his speeches. Attacking momentous issues confronting American and the world, he has delivered historical and inspiring orations that are captured in this new book. Alan Gottlieb has selected President Bush's most pivotal speeches to be enjoyed for a lifetime.

JUST MAIL IN OUR SIMPLE-TO-USE FORM HERE TO ORDER COPIES, OR CALL: (425) 454-7009

DISCOUNT SCHEDULE

1 COPY	$9.95	25 COPIES	$150.00
5 COPIES	$40.00	50 COPIES	$275.00
10 COPIES	$65.00	100 COPIES	$500.00

Please send me_____copies of *GWB Speaks to the Nation*. Enclosed is my check or money order in the amount of $_____.

Please charge my: ☐Visa ☐Mastercard ☐AMEX ☐Discover

Number: _____Expires: _____

Signature:_____

Print Name: _____

Street: _____

City: _____ **State:** _____ **Zip:**_____

Phone: (_____)_____

Mail to: Merril Press, PO Box 1682, Bellevue, WA., 98009

WOULD YOU LIKE MORE COPIES OF

THE HANDGUN IN

PERSONAL DEFENSE?

JUST MAIL IN OUR SIMPLE-TO-USE FORM HERE TO
ORDER MORE COPIES!

-OR-

CALL (425) 454-7009!

DISCOUNT SCHEDULE

1 COPY	$15.00	25 COPIES	$250.00
5 COPIES	$67.00	50 COPIES	$425.00
10 COPIES	$120.00	100 COPIES	$800.00

Merril Press
P.O. Box 1682
Bellevue, WA 98009

Please send me_____copies of *The Handgun in Personal Defense.*
Enclosed is my check or money order in the amount of
$_____.
Please charge my: ☐Visa ☐Mastercard ☐AMEX ☐Discover

Number: _____**Expires:** _____

Signature:_____

Print Name: _____

Street: _____

City: _____ **State:** _____ **Zip:**_____

Phone: (_____)_____